HOW TO FAIL IN BUSINESS

How To Fail In Business

150 Successful Methods

Troy Dowden

Writers Club Press
New York Lincoln Shanghai

How To Fail In Business
150 Successful Methods

All Rights Reserved © 2002 by Troy Dowden

Writers Club Press
an imprint of iUniverse, Inc.

For information address:
iUniverse, Inc.
2021 Pine Lake Road, Suite 100
Lincoln, NE 68512
www.iuniverse.com

2nd Edition
No pencils were harmed during the writing and printing of this publication

ISBN: 0-595-25735-6 (pbk)
ISBN: 0-595-65293-X (cloth)

Printed in the United States of America

Contents

Foreword

"What the…?! How did you get in here? Get outta my office and take that trash with you!"

—Literary Agent (Unnamed)

Prologue
FAILURE—THE NEW FRONTIER

Here's a new thought. The average person's definition of failure and success is dead wrong. But you may quadrifrattically ask, "What then is 'failure'?" Aren't the closed shops, empty offices and halted startups considered "failures" while contrasting images like expansions, franchises and "Entrepreneur Of The Year" awards considered "successes"? Not any more.

To understand failure, one must understand the stress/release continuum. Stress is a natural part of life that we *don't* want. Many people, however, will pay nine dollars to see a person driven to his physical and emotional limits, jump out of a burning building to save his wife and stop a bunch of international bad guys from stealing six hundred million dollars of negotiable bearer bonds rather than face up to the real-life stress of a tax audit. Why are people willing to pay to see, read or hear about other persons enduring highly stressful situations rather than experience it themselves? Because they know that stress can syncopate one's quiddilative functions—in other words, make them very, very sick. So they do their utmost to avoid it.

Which takes us to the purpose of this book: to help those in the business field avoid the sickifying stress of trying to succeed which brings along with it the added risk of an untimely demise (not to mention the horde of lawyers that will appear from out of nowhere). And not just business owners need to learn this. There are those in the entertainment field, the computer field, service-oriented fields and other fields that feel this stress. These too have become so successful that they have no more peace! They're so busy handling pressing engagements that when they do finally come home their spouse calls them "resident" by mistake. They can't even go for quiet walks to the corner for their morning asparagus frappuccino without the paparazzi turning it into a snap-a-thon. These ones too need to fail in order to regain their peace. But you may be wondering, "Does it make sense for one to plan to fail?" Yes indeed. If you've ever been skiing you know exactly what we're talking about. The chief reason why people break their bones from skiing is because they try so hard not to! As any ski expert can tell you, to avoid breaking limbs, one needs to *learn how to fall!* And that is what we're providing you: key information to help you to not only fail, but to fail in style.

So to add to the release quorum of our equation, failure is indeed the *new frontier*. It makes for stress free living. Some measure success by the money they make for themselves and their respective industries. But is it really success if all peace and tranquility is gone? Is it really success if your privacy is virtually non-existent? Here is true success:

Brian Lacontropy
Jester Willimton
Mi'chelle Deboulevard

Who are they? We don't know. Do you know them? Probably not. But do they care? Definitely not. Why? Because they are true success-fullers: NO stress, NO backstabbing, NO tabloid exposes…NO myo-cardial infarctions, NO ulcers…they enjoy complete and utter unadulterated peace.

Now keep in mind how this book is *not* to be used. It is not to encourage lawsuit-prompting activities. This book was published for budding (and soon to be dudding) entrepreneurs, business owners and professionals. If done properly, everyone, from employees to clients to fans will slowly but surely slink or even run away from you leaving you by yourself in unhindered bliss.

And isn't that where you want to be? Allow your mind to flow creatively as you devise the demise of your business. As you do this, realize that you are not only expanding your mind's limits, but you're helping your workers, employees, partners, investors and fans to follow your vision with you. Some 139,402 businesses failed last year. Wouldn't it be nice to be part of those astonishing statistics? Well, the creator of Cornercopia and "Toby-the Movie" with the assistance of the publisher of AnimePlus and Japartrey have brought you the most successful steps to failure. Have you heard of these ventures? NO, of course not! And that's why we're the right ones to put together this groundbreaking book.

As professionals of failure, we have compiled over 150 phenomenal points that are worth remembering and will *guarantee* you failure every time. These creative, time-tested methods and ideas are so effective that anyone and everyone that does business with you will scatter in haste. Along with personal insights from the author, it also makes for a rather pleasant cure for insomnia.

The hustle, bustle and stress of success is not worth the paper it's written on. Why add all these omnisiquous factors to your life? Failure is the key. Less stress. No striving to excel. No fighting to sit in with the big boys and learn big boy talk. No struggling to be recognized as a "potential money man." Ahh. The sweet smell of failure will keep you smiling all the way to the...er...um...who needs that expression anyway?

So sit back relax and get ready for the key elements of failure. Don't forget to tell your friends and family.

From the Publishers

1

Office Basics

To start us off, let's begin from the very core: the office setting. From here has grown many a business. But happily too, many a failure was started in that good ole office. We will carefully examine different aspects of the office setting and see which areas need to be adjusted in order to fail successfully.

TAKE THE SPLUNGE

You know what you want to do and you know how you want to do it. Jump into it. How? There are a couple of ways.

Take everything you have and buy that office furniture that you saw so elegantly displayed in your neighbor's catalog (which somehow, accidentally found it's way onto your coffee table). What some new business starters do wrong is that they live out of a paper bag. They get the office, they get the staff, but they don't live like they "own the place." How can the business starter solidify to those around him that it's *his* business, his dream, that he's the "big cheese"? He can't do this convincingly if his desk set up is comprised of an empty three-gallon paint container and an empty washing machine box-like a big rat worked there (which is taking the "big cheese" moniker too far).

So take those first few borrowed bucks and start from the top. What about a large desk with an Italian leather "money" chair that is so large you have room for an extra behind? As a soon-to-be executive you want to feel power. Nothing says power like a Rolex watch (and even after chapter 11 proceedings force you to pawn it you can still show off the indentation left on your wrist). What about the new 3500mhz computer that's out? It's so powerful it causes the sun to blink every time you turn it on, and so fast it's three words *ahead* of you as you type. You can even add these necessities:

• "You The Man" screensaver

• Shoe ionizer

• Monogrammed contact lenses

• 65-ink pen (shoulder harness included)

• Pager cuff links

• Gary Coleman sings Sting CD

After you get these amenities, you can then use the little cash left over and get other pseudo-necessary things (e.g. phones, front door, furniture, running water, etc.). But at least you have everything you want. Now you can not only be the boss, you can look the part!

To File or not to File

There was this one woman who saved each receipt she accumulated for SEVENTEEN YEARS! Imagine that. By that time, most of those stores were probably out of business while the others may have been taken over by big money mergers. And consider the hassles. Every receipt needs a number of calorie-burning steps to accomplish the filing process:

• Get receipt

• Put into purse (wallet, receipt envelope, etc.)

- Carry around receipt with you until you have access to file (extra weight)

- Take out receipt (risking paper cut)

- Go through each file to see where receipt goes, find it and stuff.

Imagine doing that ALL the TIME? And that's just an individual's schedule...imagine a business! Thousands of receipts per day. And don't forget the other addition...inputting it into a computer! The time wasted just waiting for a file to open can add up to hours upon hours each month. The horror. More wasted time! Then of course there's the mental anxiety..."What if Mr. Popsmorty, the inept head office manager, loses my files?"; "What if the Tasmanian Midget virus corrupts my computer rendering me helpless and leaves simulated Dodo feathers on my screen?"; "What if I have an item to return but to retrieve the receipt for it I have to battle the dreaded file gargoyles that inhabit the basement region?"

So to spare the unwanted calorie loss and headaches...don't file. Now, this is not an easy thought. One must ascend to a higher than average mental level to feel at peace with the thought of not filing. So, for those amateurs that feel that they at least need to have their receipts in one place...here's one approach:

Receipt Sculptures
File It Products Inc.
$34.95

This is an interesting concept that we found after much research. For some strange reason this home/business receipt sculpture kit was never brought to market so we have dozens of them for sale.

The beauty of this kit is that individuals need only to put the kit's special adhesive on their receipts and apply them to one of five molds. In no time the receipts will cover the mold and reveal an attractive house or animal. But, importantly, make sure that each month's receipts are a *different* animal or house model so that there isn't any confusion. Sculpt away!

TO BE OR NOT BE (AVAILABLE, THAT IS)

To meet the level of dimsality that you crave, which would be more effective: To hire more than is necessary or to hire less staff than is needed? This has been an age-old question. Early Traptoriates (an indigenous, nomadic-tribal structure that lived in the NE pre-colonized Idaho rain forest 1455 B.C.E), in their effort to go bankrupt (*reemate'li*-Traptorieze) as part of their business maturity training, would use the Not Be approach in order to fail faster. But over the years the answers have been marred by new technology and fresher methods for financial demise. Which would bring failure faster and cleaner? Well it depends on this all-important equation: Efficiency/Budget Protocol:

Eff. = 34(-2) x Budget = 12   -78/45 * 85%
Rate of rec =45.9(%6)   = 49,234 (*f*)

Precisely. Just as the above equation shows, hiring too many people raises your costs like a thermometer during a Houston summer. This would have a domino effect on other areas of business: prices go up for basic services and products. Imagine the surprise on your customers' faces if your soda shop charged a five dollar admissions fee and sold straws for $1.20 in addition to the $13.00 price for a 16oz watered down soda filled with ice. That would definitely get them running the other way to the nearest store (or bring their own straw if they're on the frugal side).

But the opposite is also true as the above equation clearly shows. Depending on how you limit your staff, if masterfully done, you should be able to bring your consumers to a boil. A ratio of 1:10 (one person to 10 fuming customers) would be apropos. This would be most effective in a service-oriented job. Imagine the faces of the customers as the lone worker walks out of the back room (after one of his regular 15 minute every half-hour breaks) and selects his next customer based on their aesthetic appeal and obvious hatred for modern fashion.

Ultimately, you have to make the call. But keep in mind your ultimate focus…the speedy end of success!

NICHE?

Niche smiche! Why do we have to always do what the market likes? Why do we always have to provide what people are looking for? Why do we always have to beat our brows with market research, consumer polls, buy/age/target/stats? Got an idea? Go for it! Whether people want it or not it doesn't matter. *You* like it don't you? At least you have one guaranteed buyer, yourself! How many niche market manufacturers can make a product and guarantee one sale? Here are some ideas that should not be hindered from reaching the consumer level:

> **Recycled Tissue**—"Achoo! Hey. This tissue feels familiar."
> **Book Rester**—Rest your book on it!
> **Reversed soda cans**! —Drink from the bottom!
> **$19.99 dollar bill**—For purchasing products advertised on TV
> **DeadAlready Batteries**—For those who don't like surprises
> **Plant Bowties**—Be the snazziest of the natural world
> **Pencil massager**—Keeps pencils straight!
> **Book Closer**—For those tired of closing books
> **My First Phlebotomy**—Tots 2-5 learn the fine aspects of this craft
> **My First Lawsuit**—Teach your children to play lawyer
> **Remote Control Pencil Sharpener**—Need we say more?

PROCRASTINATION PROS

Deadline, deadline, deadline! How do you honestly feel about deadlines? Now, be honest, candid and open. Imagine this situation: You have one day to meet a deadline but actually need three days to finish. What happens? You start the morning knowing that you need all the required information by the end of the day no ifs, ands or buts. You envision that day as being the epitome of smoothness, everything working like a well oiled machine. And you had it all planned out: Call person A, person B, person C and person D. A will send you the faxed material two minutes after you call. Person B will call your client to give you the approval to finish product. Person C will be at the ending location to okay incoming shipment. Person D will be sent all written approvals which tells the higher ups that all is finished in time with the deadline. Whew! That's the way it *should've* worked.

But what does reality dictate? Person A is out sick. But to your relief Person A has designated a replacement: but, sadly, it's The Replacement from Venus! Replacement A is so confused that he calls your company four different names including your competitor's. He puts you on hold for forty minutes before finding your file. The fax machine at Replacement A's office is not working, and their Nabisco "do-it-yourself" email program malfunctions. You call Person B to let them know that the approval is good as done. Person B quotes out of the Client/Program Quad II rulebook (page 124 par. 12F) stating the unlawfulness of over the phone non-fax approvals. You call Person A again, but you're put on hold to the sound of silence for a half-hour. A voice comes on that perks you up, but it's only telling you that the number you dialed is wrong. Oh brother. Will your week ever be the same? No. Why? Deadlines.

But, procrastination.... The sweet sound of it. Put it off. Put it off. Put it off. Push aside the deadlines. Clear away the fatigue and potential psychoanalyst visits. Leave a message on your machine as you take your first 2 hour break (right before lunch) of the day. The project will get done, maybe by you or maybe by a competitor, but in the meantime, enjoy that margarita!

CUSTOMER SERVICE

Customer service is the core of any business. It keeps customers coming back again and again. Companies, like Dell and Compaq, pride themselves on their customer service. So it is no coincidence that these companies also hold solid leads in the computer sales/production divisions nationwide and worldwide respectfully. This being the case, it is the perfect area to thwart.

Customer service is handled in different ways. We'll target some of these:

The Human Touch—Somebody's got to do it. Somebody's got to deal with your client over the phone. Don't go for the professional, courteous, patient, 20-line handling receptionist. Go for the impatient, cantankerous, never heard of touch-tone, too hard-core for Navy Seals, straight from the edge receptionist. Why? Because they can give your clients what they don't want: attitude. An example of your perfect phone answerer in action:

Margaret:	Hello.
Client:	Hello, I'm trying to return a computer part I purchased from you last week.
Margaret:	Who are you? I never met you.
Client:	From your company.
Margaret:	Oh. What's wrong with it?
Client:	It's broken.
Margaret:	Just like that? Maybe you put it in wrong.
Client:	No. In fact I didn't even put it in. It came in the Styrofoam in pieces.
Margaret:	Oh, I see. You didn't glue it together.
Client:	Glue? That's not my job.
Margaret:	Mine either, but that's how they go out.
Client:	That was nowhere in the instructions.
Margaret:	Yes it was, in Greek.
Client:	Greek?!

Margaret:	Are you insulting me? My great grandfather's third cousin's nephew's aunt's next door neighbor is Greek!
Client:	N-no…I just want to return this product.
Margaret:	Stick it in the mail.
Client:	What is the address?
Margaret:	No address, just stick it in.
Client:	How will it get to you?
Margaret:	I don't want it, maybe your mailman will like the treat. They work hard you know.
Client:	What about my guarantee? You better honor my guarantee!
Margaret:	Which guarantee? We have many…
Client:	On your ad. The guarantee on your ad!
Margaret:	Oh, that guarantee…what does it say?
Client:	It looks like it says 1-year guarantee on parts and labor.
Margaret:	No, look closer.
Client:	This is so small, you probably got it for free-it says…oh. Free pants and labels?
Margaret:	That's right. We got a whole box here. I believe the 70s look is in now. You have a choice of boot legs, PVC corduroys, men's Thigh Hugger® capris—
Client:	I don't believe this.
Margaret:	No, it's for real, what's your size?
Client:	You have got to be kidding.

Margaret:	Not at all. It keeps our customers happy.
Client:	[Click]
Margaret:	Hello? I guess he wanted the labels instead.

Or you can help someone perfect their craft. How often do individuals get a chance to practice their skills on others? Mark, an upcoming comedian, for example would appreciate this opportunity:

Mark:	Hello?
Client:	Yes, I have a couple questions about this product I bought.
Mark:	Don't you just hate it when the product you bought just doesn't work?
Client:	Er, ah, yeah. Well, I received the Doohickie Remover yesterday and-
Mark:	I tell you, you wonder if the store is looking at you through some binoculars, waiting till you're really happy and then press a destruct button to blow up your product.
Client:	Ah, yeah, well I would like to return it. How can I?
Mark:	That's so funny. I was returning one item and the guy at the customer service was so ugly I just dropped it and ran. He wasn't getting my limbs.
Client:	Sorry to hear that. About my product, please?
Mark:	And that wasn't the half of it-Ms. Genghis Khan-my wife, screamed at me to get my money back. I had to go back in. Mr. Ugly As

	Sin wasn't there but this short lady was at the window. All I saw was her dandruffed scalp. She was so short—
Client:	Bye.

Or... Tim a psychoanalyst:

Tim:	Hello.
Client:	Yes, I have a couple questions about this product I bought.
Tim:	Have you always had such questions?
Client:	Er, ah, no. Only since yesterday when I found that the Doohickie Remover I received wasn't working—
Tim:	Is it a regular thing for you to blame inanimate objects and major appliances for your lot in life?
Client:	Blame inanimate objects? Major appliances? What are you talking about? I have an item that I would like to return. How can I?
Tim:	I sense an inner sadness. I believe it stems from a lack of hugs in your life. I want you to reach out and hug the closest person to you.
Client:	I want to reach out and hug your neck.
Tim:	Very good. You're allowing your feelings to come out. Let it out. Let it have free reign.
Client:	Bye.

Another variable is more heartwarming. This country is unique and wonderful in the way it opens up opportunities for immigrants to become part of American society. You can help these newcomers in their quest by giving them the receptionist position. How else can one learn American speak better than dealing with the public one on one.

For our example we will use Shagufta to show this training process in action. The best way is to have Shagufta repeat what she hears (you may need an interpreter to tell her to do this). By repeating everything she hears it would be a fine step in learning the language:

Client:	Hello?
Shagufta:	Heyyo?
Client:	Yes, I have a question about this product I bought.
Shagufta:	Ches. I yave ah qwekshun bout dis produck yiy bat.
Client:	Excuse me?
Shagufta:	Excuyame?
Client:	Is there someone that I can speak to that understands the language?
Shagufta:	Es dere sommom dat y cyan spek to day speks da leengweeg?
Client:	Oh brother (click)
Shagufta:	O brodder cleeck

Perfect. The customer wasn't able to get anywhere. But you did render a potential new American citizen a service that they (and your client) would never forget. There isn't a need for insults or expletives. Remember, you want to fail in the smoothest way possible.

And there are other budding professionals who would like their first break:

Sports Announcer
Opera Singer
Mime
Tina Yothers

Hold—But despite the ever present and jovial customer service, there is always a need to put someone on hold. Putting someone on hold allows for many important behind the scenes events to occur: looking for information that you *know* isn't there, connecting to another line, laughing at a caller's accent, pretending you're busy, rushing to turn off the radio, telling everyone in the office to keep the "Boss Is Away" party down, or even rushing a co-worker out of the office to escape the date from the Deep Lagoon. Yes. Everyone has to "hold on" from time to time. But why bore them with the sweet sound of symphonies and five-set orchestras? Why settle them with the mellow, stress-relieving tempo of jazz? We have some suggestions for sounds that can be played on hold that will definitely boost one's spirits:

Busy Signal
Baby Crying
Silence
Newlyweds arguing
Explosions
Two people whispering
Loud Maniacal Laughter
A man with a severe lisp reading War and Peace
Snoring
Screeching Fingernails on a Blackboard
Gilbert Godfreid screaming, "You're on Hold!"
A nasally English chap counting the seconds
The Russian version of "You Light Up My Life"
Estimated time on hold announcement
   ("5 hours ten minutes…5 hours nine minutes")

Because of clever undermanning and splendidly annoying work hours no one is in house. Automated messages are then an excellent method to use.

Here is an example of an appropriate message for all eager potential clients to hear:

> "Hello, no one is here right now as this monotonously cold voice is obviously telling you. Please press any button between one and six except six to get to the department you are looking for. If you have big fingers and can't press one number at a time please hang up and pick on a phone your own size."

Button	Response
#1	"Ouch! Hey pick someone else!"
#2	"Please press #6 to get transferred"
#3	"This is the personnel department. Please press #6 to continue this process."
#4	"You are in the right place" [dial tone]
#5	"Sorry, try again."
#6	"Hey! I told you not to press me! Try another number."

With all these fine customer services tips you will be well talked about in no time.

Yes. The good ole office. Don't get too used to it. With these successful tips implemented you will be officeless in no time.

2

Promote Yourself

"You build it, they will come." A famous phrase from a popular movie. But this phrase doesn't work for everyone. It didn't work for Noah and it didn't work for Ford (Edsel). So how does one get them to come? Advertise, advertise, advertise. But wouldn't advertising increase business or, in a much scarier vein, bring success (or the "s" word), if done properly? Yes, but not if done improperfloricly. We know your juices are flowing as we speak. So how can we advertise to our demise?

BETTER THAN A HOME SHOW

Why a home show? A home show can be used for practically anything these days. A couple of years ago we sent Marla, our sock coordinator, on an assignment to cover one aspiring artist's home show. He had his living room, kitchen and bedroom bedecked with his paintings and sculptures. Marla considered herself a woman of good taste (that's why we picked her), but the only thing she considered even remotely creative was the round sculpture on the living room wall. The way the light tickled this object's plastic, cream colored face reminded her of the Caribbean sands twinkling in the sun. She found out later on, to her embarrassment, that it was a thermometer (something told her she shouldn't have taken it off the wall), but at least it had class. But that was how he wanted to make himself known, through a home show. He had flyers distributed to mark this grand event and they worked. Even though there were two visitors the whole evening, that was a whopping

200% more than originally! Even more enthralling is that it went up to 300% by midnight (the maid).

A home show, though, is not unique enough or impactful enough. What home show twist would work in this florgicious 21th century? Because of the increase of gadgets everyone nowadays has the latest gadgets and a "gadget cabinet" to store them in. Gone are the days of quiet corners and empty cubby holes. Instead, you have corners jam packed with "stuff" and crevices jam packed with "overflow stuff." So how does one have a home show? Use your bathroom! Creative, isn't it? Whether you're promoting your new doohickie, or selling actual bear hair socks...the bathroom is the perfect place to showcase your wares. Think: There is always some running water for washing hands and drinking. There are also towels nearby-no running around in case you spill your New Dandelion Juice cocktail extravaganza. There is a built in podium so you can rise above the masses to make your point (plus an additional plateau for an additional speaker)...and there's the plunger in case someone wants to get rowdy. The bathroom, the new concept promotion niche.

PRESS CONFERENCE

Bring the newspapers, bring the media, bring the children. A press conference is going to be coming at ya! But how do you bring it to its zenith in inefficiency? Don't tell anyone! When you get there and you're standing on the podium, enjoy the view (and the sound of the crickets).

WEB SITES

To think. There was a time when the Internet was for the chosen few. But now, millions upon millions are ignoring abdominal pains, marriage mates, nuclear spills, the loud, piercing scream of "Where'd my nose go?" from a room somewhere in the house and are accessing the online world hourly. How can you get a piece of this pie? After much research we came up with the ultimate show stopper...

Take out a newspaper ad and put together an unbelievable, mouth watering promotion that makes individuals want to latch on to your web site (make sure it's an easy site name to remember) and leave their names and numbers to win a valuable prize. This is very simple. Don't forget to put a cut off date.

**The First 100 visitors to our site
will receive a 2003 BMW Hover!**

Hurry to our site and submit your name now!
Contest ends November 31, 2002
Log on to fill out online application:
http://www.cara-san/~modin.opt/intelli-pause*.*/68 quetin.gld./ogg-pomade~threeteir/rigoO0Omortispike.est. phila.com/

DOOR TO DOOR

Ring, ring, ring. If you want to make an impression in a potential client's mind (and carpet) the door to door methodology is the best.

The door to door approach has long been the most effective way of reaching people and successfully impacting their minds with shpeel. One man who used to work at our London office some forty years ago was a whiz at the doors. No matter what you tried to do he got the package into your hand. He always started off with a greeting but would then go right into the product presentation. For example, there was the time he was selling toothbrushes in New Jersey. The lady of the house opened the door to find him with a wide grin and his hand already extended for a handshake. This got the lady smiling. But her smile also gave away her secret…three rows of teeth. This was a rare case. Chances are this lady probably ran out of toothbrushes quite regularly. What was he to do? He went into his bag and (unbeknownst to her) put a rubber band around three toothbrushes and pulled them out. "Triple Scrub" he called it, but it worked. This woman is now a loyal customer (and one-woman traveling side show act).

So what was the point of all this? We don't know. In fact we don't even remember why we brought it up.

COLD CALLING

Cold calling over the phone is one of the hardest methods to reaching potential clients. You don't know how they look, you don't know what expression is on their face and you don't know what weapon they have in their hand. So only a few people can successfully turn a cold call into a warm sale. But there is something all of us can do. We can quicken the click. Of course, anyone can be rude and have the phone dropped mercilessly on their ears. But what's the *point if your company isn't mentioned?*

To make your quickening of the click most effective a few key items must be mentioned. Notice these vintage selections:

"Hello. My name is Troy from Goring and Charles. We are looking for people that want to trade their liver in for some really good china."

"Hello. My name is Welbourne from Art's Painting and Antiques. We'll be in the area in the next few days. Please leave your spouse on the front porch for pickup."

"Hello. This is Jerry from Jerry's Fishery. We are having a sale on sea slug sushi sandwiches."

"Hello. This is Mary with Mary's home repair. Would you like your bedroom door shrunk 30 inches and sealed permanently?"

"Hi. This is Jane from Austin's Security. We install high tech security devices in homes and offices. Can you give us your security code and the location of your valuables?

"Hello? Ms. Sow? We are from Allen's Deli. Do you eat like a pig?"

"Hello? This is Jimmy from Jim's auto repair. We promise to lie to you about fake engine damage, overcharge you for doing nothing, steal the change out of your glove compartment and give your name and address to Junk Mail America."

"Hi. This is Sherry from Earl's Exterminators. We have a sale on mystery meat sandwiches."

So we see. The cold call is a very effective method toward losing customers. Ask the right question you get the right answer. Ask away!

THE QUESTIONNAIRE

What about a questionnaire? A questionnaire is one way for us to reach customers who don't happen to walk into our office on the 22nd floor of our elevatorless building. The questionnaire also allows individuals to receive a free gift just by filling out the form.

One budding entrepreneur had a way of getting questionnaires into the hands of unsuspecting potential clients: He would put a little adhesive on the blank side and stick it on the forehead of passersby as he made his daily commute down the avenue. He would target everyone, from students to taxi drivers, from mayors to mimes. His success rate was phenomenal at .004% (which is a record for the forehead-splat method). But at times he got the right person. One man in his haste didn't notice he was "splatted" with the questionnaire until two days later. He wasn't really interested in the free gift of 3 ounces of Polly's Shine Remover, but because of the ingenuity he filled it out and received his free product five years later. This one sale ingrained this entrepreneur's product permanently in someone's mind (not to the mention the permanent glue stain on the foreheads of thousands).

Another man had a very unique method of getting his questionnaires into unsuspecting potential clients' hands: He would infiltrate delis, diners and restaurants, sneak into their kitchens and place his questionnaires into the sandwiches. Saleswise this had minimal impact but the sandwiches he "touched" became so popular he saved up his money and created "Felroy's Card Stock Eatings" which went out of business two days after its grand opening. But he was creative and that's what you need to be also.

We have one example of an effective questionnaire:

Fill out Questionnaire and receive a free thing!*
(All spaces should be filled out to receive thing)

Full Name (In Koine Greek) :_____

Age: ____ years _____ months _____ hours _____ seconds

Your Best Friend's Neighbor's Favorite Nephew's Address: _____

Telephone Number (___) ____-_____-_____-ext____

Household Income Under $234 ____   Over $189,000____

How many children 1__   3.5 ___   24 ___

Shoe size 1-9 ___   10-12 ___   13-29___   11 toes ____

If a train is going south at 45mph and another isn't what is the conductor's name? _____

Where were you on June 23, 1986 at 2:35pm? _____

Were you ever *caught* stealing   Yes ____   No ____

* Yes, a thing.

Yes. Advertise, advertise, advertise and you will get attention for yourself and your company. But, who needs that? Advertise the right way and you will be on your way to enjoying the peace of mind you deserve.

3

Business Presentation

Now you have your clients where you want them, front and center. Whether it is the meeting of the minds with three clients or twenty clients, you have the opportunity to show them what you got. You now have the opportunity to show them why they cannot go without your expertise and experience. But of course, you are geared for failure. How can you successfully turn this "eye to eye" into a "flee and run"?

TIMING MATTERS...

If you want to be successful get there on time and take a tour of the place. You need to BE your surroundings. Soak up the boss' office, his Latin leather chair and check out each cooler on the floor (did you know that the further east the cooler the more the water leans southward?). Share some jokes with the secretaries (they can always use a breather). When you get to the presentation room, take off those shoes and socks! Feel that carpet between your toes. And don't forget the foot massage. A foot massage is an effective way to take away the pre-presentation jitters. Preferably you have a partner that can do the massage for you, but if not (and their CEO says "No way!") do it yourself. But don't forget to wipe your hands off on your tie before shaking hands; etiquette, you know. Be careful, though. One presenter laid down on the presentation table and did his "roll your way to a perfect back" maneuver, but that would not be recommended. It's not professional.

THE INTRODUCTION

The name game can be rewarding or it can be a waste of time. When you get to your potential client's office and you find that you've forgotten their name, don't worry about it. Call everyone "Money." Executives like that.

Shake, shake, shake. The handshake is an interesting concept that has met worldwide acceptance as a necessary part of the introduction process. The myths surrounding the origin of the handshake can be piled miles high. From the Adriatic Plateau you hear that handshakes were used primarily to shake loose change from weary travelers. From the Yeti Peninsula you read about how the handshake was a way of releasing dormant underarm parasites. In the MidEastern Bollogrounds you hear about how these primitive people shook hands as a way of saying "Boy, wasn't that a good grub sandwich?" The use of two hands in this custom specified a double-decker. So, we really don't know where the handshake came from, but it should be used whenever you're introduced to a potential client. What kind of shake should you give? Give "Money" a real shake; strong, firm, lasting. That signifies trust. And the more you hear the bones-a-shuffling, the more his face contorts into one big, shriveled, pouted, grimace the stronger his trust in you will grow.

YOUR EQUIPMENT MATTERS!

Why spend money on the latest presentation technologies that can run you anywhere between $2,500 to $20,000 when you can do it yourself with ease and low cost. The larger the group the visually smaller the presentation should be. If you're using a slide projector, limit the amount of light utilized by projecting a 2″ x 3″ sized screen (anything smaller would be silly) on a nice white cotton bedspread taped to the wall. This will save your client money. For those businesses that have money to squander, you can try the VISCERAL approach and encompass the whole room! This procedure is visually shocking and definitely memorable. How is this done? If a projector is being used, pull back on the light until the screen zooms room size encompassing the back wall, ceiling, adjoining walls and part of the floor. Make your client read your business plan off the faces of their coworkers...visually stunning.

LET 'EM HEAR IT

The voice is an essential piece of equipment no business presentation should be without. Voice-overs get millions of dollars for just saying a few words about a movie via the trailer ("Rush and see The Runaway Shoelace Part Six") or about a dairy product ("It will make you moo!"). So the same with business presentations. Good speakers know how to balance pauses, pace and pitch, catching the audience's ears in a snare, readying them to shell out some bucks. But of course you wouldn't want that. Nasally is the way to go. The more slurred the better. Have your audience leaning, pining their ears to understand every word. This strengthens ear muscles that are rarely used. And to add a definite touch, find your speaker on the way to the presentation. Probably that young man who's counting leaves or that old lady who's feeding the pigeons while licking her bagel-on-a-stick could help out. A couple of bucks will get them to get up the nerve to speak. This would be an excellent way to train these strangers in the fine art of public speaking.

The opening line to your presentation should always be witty (unless you're using the always successful spittle-in-your-face method).

A number of key openers:

- "99 Bottles Of Beer On The Wall" (sung in full Borscht waitress dress)

- The famous forty-five minute Gretsky Waltz (leaves you about ten key minutes to do your presentation)

- How you felt about that first pimple on your nose on your first day of high school (photos would be apropos)

- If you decide to open with a joke, make sure you ALWAYS give a mighty back-bending guffaw after each liner (the longer the guffaw the better, but remember you have presentation to dismember).

A whoopee cushion has long been a tension breaker over the centuries. Why break tradition. Use one on your chair to exflirberate your point, but DO NOT OVERKILL.

The art of speaking is one skill that is taken lightly in many circles. But once the level of speak expertise is met, it can be like music to the ears of your listeners.

One man had such expertise. He could convince anyone of anything. He could convince people that he was a foot taller than his 5'-2" frame indicated and had record sales selling flats at a women's shoe store. He so thoroughly convinced customers at a jewelry store he worked at that clear Lego block engagement rings were worth more than diamonds (to the relief of male suitors). He even broke sales records at a music store by single-handedly selling two of William Shatner's Greatest Hits albums in twenty-three years. He should be getting out of jail soon, but in any case, his style was simple: illustrate, illustrate, illustrate. Did we mention illustrate? And that he did. Those who are handling the business presentation need to do just that to get the attention of their hosts. And to give them a presentation they would never forget, involve someone that your hosts know so well: their boss (who's hopefully in the audience).

We have an excerpt from one of our graduates, Donald Woodies from our night course as he, with grace and skill, shows the fine art of teaching during an actual business presentation. Note his excellent use of illustrations:

> [Donald speaking] "Yes, my company and I have a unique idea that we would like to bring to your attention. The world has been informed and is working towards the "paperless office." We want to bring to you the "papercutless office." As you notice, in my right hand and your left is a sheet of paper [raising hand]. I will now

have Mr. Beltler [the boss] forcibly brought to the front of the room to take part in this demonstration [two employees reluctantly grapple with Mr. Beltler and bring him to the front of room].

"Mr. Beltler. Thank you for your voluntary assistance."

"Grunt [grunting]."

"The pleasure is all ours. Now would you like me to take the edge of this paper and whisk it across your face?"

"You better not!" Beltler growls.

"Of course not. Because of the chance of a paper cut. But not if our Paper Bumper technology is applied. Fortran [assistant], can you bring me a sheet of our new paper?"

[Fortran brings it to Woodies]

"Our paper has around its edges a half inch thick, rounded, flexible barrier made of Fleblar, an odorless and residueless rubber-like compound which will prevent paper cuts, the number one cause of death in the office. We would now like to demonstrate how protected office staff will be with our border in place. [Fortran comes forward with an oversized, padded boxing glove]

"My assistant has on not just an ordinary boxing glove, but a glove padded with Fleblar, the same material used on our paper's borders. He will now wind up and punch Mr. Beltler..."

Time and space doesn't permit us to print all of this excellent example of a business presentation meister at work. But you should get the picture: illustrate, illustrate and illustrate.

Now, keep in mind that there are different ways to illustrate. You can bring the boss (or CEO) up in front of the room like the above example or you can use the *tushee technique* and have them squirm in their chair. One graduate caused the boss of a prospective client to squirm so much he was sued for personal property damage: pleather burns. But to get them to squirm you need to do a lot of research. Here's an excerpt from one of our graduates, Paul Thornby, at a recent business presentation:

[Paul] "Isn't it a shame that it is so hard to find men's suits that fit perfectly? You have to search here and there, find it, bring it back, complain and sue to get the right fit. And then after a couple of decades it doesn't fit anymore and you have to go shopping again. But that is the past."

[His assistant, Betty, brings a man's suit and holds it up]

"This suit is not an ordinary suit. It's called the FlexSuit-one size fits all. You may have noticed the strings that hang from the seams. These aren't ordinary strings. They're patented drawstrings that miraculously give this suit the flexibility it needs to fit any size and shape with just a light pull. Like for example, Mr. Elton [the boss]. Here is a person who has no taste in clothes. While style and fashion has changed over the years, his suits look like they were in a coma and missed that now distant "turn of the century". When he got that suit the Year 1900 compliance bug was the fear and Dick Clark was a rocking pre-schooler.

"But he grew and grew to the girth that he possesses that takes up a full one quarter of this room, but as you noticed his suit didn't grow with him. He can't button his jacket without fear of turning it into a hospital gown. The pants have 100% polyester patches to keep them together and the vest looks like its keeping in a raucous laugh. FlexSuit is the future."

Perfect. Paul paid keen attention to detail and did his research before putting on such an inspiring (and tear jerking) performance.

So we see how the method we use to teach is so essential. Illustrate through the visual, like our first example, or paint a picture with words like the second example. Make sure you use the boss or CEO for full impact and ready a nice ending to drive the point home (and you along with it).

Catch Them With Color!

Use the eyes. There are an amazing amount of colors your eyes can perceive…but did you know that grayscale is also as vast? 256,000 gray tones! Challenge your clients visually. Help them to sharpen their eye modules by using only *variations of gray* in your presentation. Force your client, for example, to see your company's bagel sales by the hour, day and month for twelve years by using a line chart that increases the grayscale 3% for every hour. And if you really want to stun them, use the same phenomenal incremental tonal range in a 3-D pie chart!

LEAVE BEHINDS

"Leave behinds" are visual take-it-from-the meeting printouts that allow your clients to leave with your presentation in hand. It's a key methodology to helping them remember what they seen and heard. But the key to ~~failure~~ success? Make sure the leave behinds have nothing to do with the presentation. Some choice options:

- Family photos (copies, of course)

- A stack of activity flyers (crosswords, connect the dots, the "get the CEO to the board meeting" maze)

- "Programming Your ColecoVision"-video tutoring

- A bag of "Connect the Shreds"

- "The Origin of Toe Jam" series" (4 volume set)

- Handwritten leave behinds by your six year old daughter on why she doesn't like school lunch will leave a touching end to your presentation.

SEND A GIFT

A gift sent by mail a few days after a presentation always means "remember me." Sending your prospects a memorable token of your appreciation can be a positive step to reacquaintance. Reacquaintance? Yucky! Any suggestions?

- His and Her Post-nuptial Kit

- Pet Sock (batteries not included)

- 30 second calling cards (10-pack)

- Bag of Jelly Beans (Cod Liver oil flavor) with chewy Fleblar center

- War and Peace Manuscript—35pt font size

- Portable Blink Counter (wink upgradeable)

- Pallet of slightly used manila folders (instructions included)

It will take some practice to really get these points well in mind, but don't give up. With practice, you will be so successful nobody will want you back, ever! A job well done.

4

Home Suite Home

With the advent of personal computers, the Desktop Publishing field has burst anew. No more do individuals need to go to the printer to do graphic work when they can now save all that money and mess up from home. And it makes sense. Why go out of your house to bring back disorganized, uncollated dribble, when you can, with ease, and comfort botch up comfortably at your own residence?

Those who are looking into the Desktop Publishing field have so many options. They can do resumes, restaurant menus, advertising, flyers and posters promoting everything from a midnight looting party to used dentures sales...the works. But how can they find the sweet smell of failure in this field?

TITLING

Penmanship. Remember the glory days when good penmanship was the goal of all children? Books were written that strengthened penmanship, with dotted lines that helped you to hold the letters steady and keep them in their correct proportional station. Laser printers and ink jets now come with fonts and pica sizes galore for titling. But don't let that stop you. You took years to get your penmanship right. Go without the coffee for a couple of days, put those contacts in backwards (to enlarge your canvas) and *freehand* your titling for posters and oversized banners (don't forget to keep your crayons inside the lines).

SPELL CHEK? WY BOTTHER?

There are proofreaders that make thousands of dollars to look over a body of work. A ten-page document may run you a couple of hundreds of dollars. But who makes the rules as to what is correct anyway? In New York we spell it "honor," while across the sea they spell it "honour." Is there a war over this? No. Why? Because *nobody cares.* In this publication you will find some words that seem strange but are just as valid as the word "moody" which has *nothing* to do with cows. So here are some choice ditties to add to your desktop publishing projects (and don't mind that red squiggly line that comes under these selections when you type them in-it's just a computer. What does it know?)

> **Flexitile**—the art of being flexible and versatile at the same time
> **splunge**—a plunge that ends in a splash (e.g. jumping into a thick river)
> **competitious**—always being competitive
> **flarmicious**—this is a blank word-use it whenever it feels right in place of words like: smelly, corny or loud.
> **dainterrier**—ever met a person who is nice one day and vicious to the point of carniverousation the next?
> **spud**—pass tense of "sped"

COPYRIGHTING/PATENT PROTECTION

Why spend $10 on copyrighting...if you can get something to eat instead? Protection of one's ideas that they have so strongly created is a necessary thing. But if you were stuck on a deserted island and you had a choice between that copyright or a steak on rye with all the trimmings, which would you pick? No question.

What about a patent? Yeah, the naysayers practically swear by its use and they have a minor point: protect yourself. But have you ever looked around and saw how many legal rip-offs are out there? For example, how many Ab-xx machines are out there to bomb, boost, bojangle and beckon your abs into a chiseled, washboard look? Don't they all look and act the same? Weren't they also patented? Ah ha! So then, if you patent, all someone has to do is make a minor adjustment and, wallah! Competitiousness. You can't help but feel so sorry for the guy that invented the hamburger. Now there are twenty thousand different hamburgers out there. Some are flame-broiled, others are steamed, others are chewy with a crunchy, toasted maggot center. But each has a little zing that makes it different and once again, competitious. And let's take this step further. What if your product is protected by the patent and someone comes up with a similar idea? Would you be willing to spend days, weeks or even months fighting in the court system to block the sale of, for example, the Widgetoid product which closely resembles your Wijetoid except for the widget spring on the top? So instead of wasting the $800–$15,000 to patent, why not invest in some good stock. Here are some options:

Deetratel (DeL)
Manufacturer of SpringThings© flower-patterned bed springs.
Company Slogan: "You can't see em, but you know they're there."

Prinking Publishing (PgP)
Produces I Tee!© software that counts the number of 't's' in a written work.
Company Slogan: "Software for the rest of us."
Hot Stock tip! Look for I Jay! software in 2003.

HefemUp (Hep)
Manufacturer of NatureCrunch© Shoes that sound an audible "Ouch" as you walk. Company Slogan: "Remember our Friends the ants."

ReChew Bros. (ReC)
Manufacturer of ReChew© recycled gum.
Company Slogan: "Cleaner streets and a healthy jaw—a perfect combination."

Ahhhh! (AhH)

Manufacturers of Sweat In a Can®—They believe that there's no better way to replace lost fluids than with 100% sweat.
Company Slogan: "You lose it, reuse it!"

I See You (ICU)

No Bibs Needed©. This company pioneered the first restaurant where customers are fed intravenously.
Company Slogan: "Burpless eating—the future of fine dining"

TalkAway (GE)

Maker of extensions cords for home phones. 300ft, 400ft and 800ft lengths available.
Company Slogan: "We're putting the cellular phones out of business."

On Time Products (OT)

Year 3,000 A.D. countdown clock.
Company Slogan: "Keeps on ticking, even though you can't."

EQUIPMENT

Sharp, exciting, stimulating printouts…eye-catching, thought provoking, captivating visuals. Why bother? You could spend hundreds to thousands of dollars on color ink jet printers and color laser printers, but who needs them. Save money and also get the smooth, titillating sound of a 9-pin dot matrix black and white printer. Yes, it will take all day to print a five page document with graphics, but think of the warm tat-tat-tat sound, the savings and the jaggies. In fact, a survey of 46 business men and women was taken to note what sounds put them to sleep the fastest. Here are the surprising results that were noted (in order of least to greatest):

10. The sound of a person in corduroys walking

9. The gentle whisper of a catalytic converter

8. The smargled buzz of a bee in honey

7. A starched shirt

6. The words "whole wheat doughnut"

5. The boss closing his office door

4. Their neighbor saying "home movies"

3. The words "diet hot fudge sundae"

2. The phrase "staff meeting"

1. The sound of a 9 pin dot matrix printer

So we see. If you want to retrofy that home office and also keep it a place of calmness (and drowsiness) 9-pin it!

GUARANTEE

Your word is your bond. Forget the hassles of written agreements, the burden of contractual obligations. This country was built on a handshake. Let your customer know that you are a man of your word (just don't tell them which one). Promise your customer what you'll give them: their work back. But as for timing, can you really promise that an emergency vacation wouldn't arise causing you to flee the country and miss the deadline next week Tuesday? Can you really guarantee that you'll have their work back, collated and organized, with all the inter-office hurricanes that are rampant? Can you really know if your 16-year old equipment will survive another power up? It wouldn't be fair or practical to make any promises. In fact it would be downright dishonest.

So tell them, simply put, "We'll call you when it's ready." No dishonesty, no pipe dreams, no fluff, straight out honesty. If they would like to call you to find out more information give them this universal number (800) 279-452 (make sure to use these on all advertising).

additional numbers: 1 (888) 456-343
                          1 (800) 788-902

COLLATING

What is collating? It is the continual, rigid, strict, repetitive stacking of a copying or printing assignment. B-o-r-i-n-g. Give your customers a life. Help them to see that variety is the spice of life. Should page 3 always come before page 4? Imagine this intriguing concept…5, 12, 45, 2, 9! Wow, don't you feel relieved, refreshed, released from the rigid, organizational 1-2-3 format. Imagine your client's exubilation! Another release from the collatial bind: why do three-hole punched documents need their holes lined up vertically? Challenge the skeptics: It would be more attractive if the middle hole was moved to the right two inches. Who's to say that this wouldn't add life to a vertically challenged document? Of course, the skeptics would. But would you tell Picasso to move the woman's eyes in his paintings to a more "normal" setting? The horror. Experiment, explore, branch out…and bring your client for the ride!

STAPLING

Imagine how you would feel if your foot had to be tied by a rope to a stake in the middle of your yard. Yes, you could move, but not far and without variety-forced to take in the unmoving unchanging visual perspective. Now imagine how stapled documents feel…listen to this ode to the stapled sheets (author unknown):

> *Click…I felt it.*
> *The icy shafts pierced my shoulder*
> *slowing me to a drawl*
> *Yes I could curl up and take a peek at the world around me,*
> *but I continue to yearn for the freedom of the newsprint*

the New York bird as I call him…flying freely,
touching lamppost, tinkling bare ankles
in the morning breeze
Newsprint has seen places I have never seen…
touched areas I have never touched,
and the joy of being stepped on by multinational toes,
while waiting to be gusted up again.
But alas I stay, stapled shoulder to shoulder with other victims
never to move, never to fly, never to roam…

Touching, wasn't it? Your clients may want that staple on the upper left, but *your paper doesn't.* **Think about the paper.** Your client just may feel the same way. If not, copy this poem and share it with them. If they aren't moved by it, they're probably totally normal.

Yes. We do yearn at times to work from home and juggle the work load, while juggling the housework, while juggling the personal phone calls, while juggling the neighbor visits and juggling salesmen visits. But take it from the Famous Barconi who used to juggle knives, axes, wine glasses, eggs (natural enemies of wine glasses) and chain saws…"RUN!"

5

Motivational Thoughts

They say a picture is worth a thousand words. And it's true. For example, "Who hung that garbage on my wall?!" But a picture can also be a daily help in keeping our goals clear in mind. Ancient Binopopocrians who inhabited the once snowy Florida coasts were well known for their use of pictures to communicate to each other. In 1209 a giant skeccipod (early equivalent to our *sketch pads*) was unearthed and it showed the amazing penmanship of this early tribe and proved that early man was indeed intelligent and no different from us today. Their god was Hotdogotos who was later defeated by the nearby Musterd tribe whose god was Heiinzzz. These early battles were also drawn on clay tablets. But these tablets barely survived to this day due to the clay tablet eating fad of 1303.

Even now, pictures are a key element to teaching. You may still recall how you were taught the alphabet, swing dancing and light engine repair through the pictures you were shown in kindergarten. Take the following phrases, blow them up and place them on your office wall. Look at them. Picture them. Motivate.

Motivational Words

If it could be done today-then it could be done tomorrow-for whence tomorrow comes it becomes a today-then we can puteth it off again

Don't put off what you can do today tomorrow-practice putting off a week's worth of work for the following month

Early bird misses on sleep

Try, try again until you unsucceed

Warning: Practice makes perfect

The customer's always right, until they open their mouths

Alas what point perfection, if there are no mess ups to compare them to?

Patience is a virtue-teach your client

Sleep, it is your best friend

Efficiency costs jobs

6

So, You're the Boss

Being the boss, the big man, El Honcho of a budding or established business venture has its benefits. You have the power to put a team of players together that will get the job done, close the deal and bring in the cash. So a motivating boss, an encouraging boss, a know-when-its-time-to-do-business boss, is the best boss to have…that is, unless you want to fail. If your workers are too happy, that makes for success. So how can bosses clamp down on this potential, but hurdleable road-block? We have for you some timeless options. Note: Though bosses come in a variety of sizes, shapes and chromosome counts (e.g. male, female, pygmidgitoid, etc.) this chapter comigulates all these varieties into a male vector to pay homage to the masculine paper used by the publishers. But bosses of the non-male persuasion can also successfully use these points.

THE NAME GAME

Call each worker by a name you've selected based on their dominant qualities. This may be a physical description or a name that signifies their unique "skills." This is a fine way to showcase to all each worker's individuality. Remember, the more honest the better. Here are some popular choices—

Mister or Miss:

Nosehair	Gums
Sameshirt	Lostfiles
Sloppydesk	Lovehandles
Eyeshadow	Cantfindaspouse
Lateagain	Tooth

Or you can give them names that are easier to pronounce than that embarrassing contraption of a name they've been wielding all these years. Now, don't get tepid about the thought of changing an employee's name, because, if you think about it, it just may be a relief to them. Why? Because the name they have was chosen and given to them *without their permission* (which explains all that fetal kicking in the womb). Not only that, they had to go through the confusion of figuring out which name was theirs amid the multiplicity of "cutesy" names they were called as infants (e.g. "snotty" "sillytoes" "booboo" etc). Jenna, on our staff, after all these years, still gets up, looks around and cries, "Moommy?" when she hears the name, "Stinkypants." So, relieve your employees from their cerebral confinement. Adjust their names and see how they react (with apologies to those whose names resemble the adjusted name):

Jeniffer Reynolds	-Beglennifer Benolds
Marty Binum	-Martybinum (with a deep southern drawl)
Richard Mortimer	-Richie Moooorrrrrrtmer (long "moo" and a strong trill on the 'r')
John Wiggins	-Hey you
Christopher O'Neal	-Christeen
Dawna Charles	-Gunther

These are guaranteed to prompt a smile (and heated whispers in the lunchroom).

WHO DA' MAN?

You can even insist upon maintaining these corporate standards:

> A salute

> Male curtsy

> Have employees pave your path with legal paper as you walk

You can even add the following to your repertoire:

> While looking upward reminiscingly, start off all your sentences with, "As the pockadoodle said to the mimibird…"

> The employee all time favorite if-I-look-over-your-shoulder-as-you-work-my-nosehairs-tickling-your-shoulder-with-hot-no-breath-mint-breath-intact-it-would-help-you-to-be-more-efficient procedure.

> Learn to burp in four languages (make sure to make one a romance language)

Or…

HAVE AN EMPLOYEE DAY

This day will be most memorable. This is an opportunity for you and your employees to dress and imitate the honored employee. The staff could wear, for example, exaggerated replicas of Jocelyn's wig (worn off-kilter by her customary 25 degrees) on one day, Marvin's plaid shirt with the yellowed 6-inch butterfly collar another day, and Billy's famous two-tone slacks with the iron imprint the following week. Replicating Bartholomew's duct-tape-peeking-out-at-the-ankles style showcases his unique tailoring skills and imitating his efforts to stick the tape back in while hopping on one foot showcases his physical dexterity. But if the staff can come up with a replica of Joanne's permanently coffee-stained blouse, make sure they don't forget to parrot her weekly, "how did that stain get there?" with the mock surprise she does so well and imitate her futile efforts to *once again* clean the spot. Be careful, though. With the whole office having the Benneefa inspired, "no eyebrows just pencil" look, work may not get done. Whatever the case, your employees will know that they are noticed.

GET TOGETHER

The team meeting is always a way to strengthen forces, collaborate on new ideas and identify purpose and structure. Employees are encouraged to give a piece of their mind as to post project observations, upcoming next steps and company direction. By listening wholeheartedly to their suggestions and responding favorably you instill and encourage company esteem. Bah! After an employee expresses their observations respond in one of these gems of a way:

> "Who wrote that for you?"
> "Did you actually waste a brain cell to say that."
> "Now, wasn't that a waste of carbon-dioxide."
> "Next!"
> "Can someone please explain why Teeth thought that necessary to say?"
> "Oh, sorry. I didn't mean to give you the impression that I cared."
> "Now, wasn't that a cure for insomnia."
> "I'm gonna throw up."

Or cut them off in mid-sentence with these classics:

> "-Sorry, time's up."
> "-Next!" (multiversal)
> "-Oops, were you speaking to me?"
> "-Ehhhhhh, wrong answer."
> "-Sorry, I didn't mean for you to speak your answer, a mind meld would have done."

Or after the comment respond with these witty actions…

> Put on a "why did you insult me like that?" face and start blubbering

> Get up and bend as far as you can backwards and hold your stomach, letting out a mighty guffaw.

> Start to wimper, sniffle and cry, "you're fired."

> Stare at them unblinkingly.

You will sure to be the talk of the town and the motivation behind the occasional burning effigy.

MONEY TIME!

Pay time is a very important time in a worker's life. Their abilities and strengths are summed up in a weekly or bi-monthly stipend. But wouldn't your workers enjoy having their weaknesses likewise summed up in their checks?

Send each worker a note emphasizing why certain amounts of money have been held back. Remember, honesty is the best policy.

$56 held back…	"Lack of corporate scent."
$112 held back…	"2 minutes late in eight months, setting bad example."
$45 held back…	"unclear as to when to laugh at boss' joke. Retraining necessary."
$89 held back…	"If it wasn't for your face, you would be pretty."
$74 held back…	"Can't salute straight"
$324 held back…	"Oops."
$29 held back…	"Didn't beat boss' Solitaire score."

LET THEM KNOW

Your workers thrive on compliments and evaluations as does any other pseudo-human. These words of wisdom and praise need to be well thought out to have the desired affect.

> "Mary. Thank you for a slob well done."
>
> "Chester, it was a pleasure messing up with you."
>
> "Jerome. How could this business survive without you? Wait. We're gonna find out next week."
>
> "Mitchell. The job you did on the Molar account was a vision of decadence."
>
> "Thanks for working those extra hours last week. You owe me."
>
> "You remind me of me when I was young, just before I got fired from my first job."
>
> "Instead of giving you all a raise, petty paper money, I have a case of Lax-o-creme in the office for everybody. You can thank me later."
>
> "Ornwell, you did a good job, but I have one suggestion. Quit."

At times thoughtful gifts say it all:

• A pen with double-click action

• Color pen (exceptional employee)

• Monogrammed erasers

• Paper clip remolder

• Paperweight holder

• A brand new shining 286 PC

• Vic 20 (with software)

• Karaoke tapes of you in Japan

• Copies of each worker's bloopers (vintage)

- Tape of each worker getting yelled at

- Slug farm (with Slime-Away for escapees)

- Butterfly attractor

- Self Tickling Machine

POSITIONS POSITIONS

A title can mean a lot. You probably think that your employees wouldn't appreciate such a nice, though empty, gesture. But think again. Didn't you feel good when you got that new title many moons ago? You still liked it even though it didn't mean anything new: same assignment, same pay (unless you were fortunate enough to get that extra 40 cents per year windfall) and the office bully still messed with your hair. But you felt good about the fact that you had ascended above the ranks of "Misc." Well, give your employees titles. Let them know to what extent you appreciate their efforts and how the title bestowed upon them is a symbol of their fortitude through stress and their diligence through projects:

Washcloth Collating Executive
Head Cubicle Commissioner
Executive of Half-Bilingual Studies
Subboss (gets the bologna heroes)
Lint Buster
Head Misc

GIVE THEM AN ASSIGNMENT

Employees like to be given assignments. They're not kids by any stretch of the imagination, but like kids being sent on a search assignment by a parent, there's a feeling of usefulness and responsibleness. Give your employees a search assignment and see how they're affected. Have them search for:

Decaffeinated erasers
Ream of one hole punched paper
Cinnamon flavored duct tape
Ball Point Pens (plaid ink only)
Road and Track magazine ("Scratch & Sniff" edition)
Bearskin Ties

EVALUATION TIME

A total evaluation of your employees would not be complete if these technological advances aren't put into working process in your office:

Pix-o-Phone
JT Flockers
This allows the boss to pick up any line his workers are on and broadcast it office wide (nationwide option included).
$45.99

Match-me-Now
Date Synopsis industries
This clever chart, which should be displayed once a month, dictates for the whole office to see, who is with whom at present, who is thinking about whom at present, and who was dumped by whom previously. Set brilliantly in "family-tree" format.
$73.22

ReMemo
Tri-Blip Techs
Wouldn't it be nice if you had a musical reminder to alert you to call your employees for "one more before you go" assignments at up to two minutes before they leave for the day? This is it. Five motion detectors included.
$12.99

The Always Away Phone

Sneak Up Industries

With high tech faux static, realistic interference blips and optional surf/
breeze sounds you always sound like you're states away (or continents
away with R72331 upgrade) when in reality you'd be right outside the
office.

$207.99

Working example:

> "How you guys doing? I'm enjoying myself here in Hawaii (sound
> of ocean waves). See you when I get in"-<after entering office> "I'm
> in!"

TEST THEIR PATIENCE

Patience is essential. With the way the world is going, the patient person will stand up far above the masses. But how would a boss know if
his employees have the required patience and inner strength needed for
their rapidly approaching job search? Test it.

> Intercom an employee five times every twenty minutes for an hour.

> Spit shine the head of any bald employee (male preferred) each
> time you meet.

> Each time you see the female employee with the mold on her nose,
> stare for four minutes at it before speaking (if she's sensitive, cut
> the staring down a minute).

> Laugh at everything a particular employee says, no matter what.

> Whisper an onion, garlic and chitlin sandwich-enhanced joke to
> your employee.

STAND LIKE A MAN

The stance of one in control is a stance above every other stance; firm, confident, ready to carry the staff on his mighty shoulders (or in the case of a woman boss, mighty shoulder pads). Just look at the statue in front of the United Nations or the stance of the Statue of Liberty. What about the stance of Bob's Big Boy? Control, power, boldness. These are the words that spring to our minds. What do you give off when you stand? "Banana"? "Weeping Willow"? Does the word "Dopey" come to mind? Set yourself apart from the beckoning fray. Create a Boss pose of your own that doesn't destroy your already stunted vertebrae. This should visually help all on your staff to remember who the leader is…who the top dog of this fashion is…unequivocally. But where to stand? An age old question that can only be answered in an age old way…"it doesn't matter, you run the joint!"—(Vesuviron 67 B.C.E)

> In front of lunch room
> at the punch in/out clock
> in front of the board meeting room
> in front of your office
> on your desk akimbo

As a boss you have the upper hand in teaching and training your employees at their own expense. Treat them right and they will gradually, one by one leave. And when your final employee is out using the last of his 3 annual vacation/personal/holiday/sick days, use the quiet time to do something you haven't done in a while:

> Skip around the office

> Take out your Mr. Rogers Neighborhood sweater and sneaks and talk to the "camera"

> Practice what you learned on the Opera Channel

Practice your "Cool Man Slick Brooklyn Style Can't Touch Me Yo Kid" bop walk across the room (with doo rag and shades)

Say, "I don't ever want to hear the word 'Mammy' again!" at the top of your voice in the nasally tone of your last client's CEO.

Pretend you're a baby, crawl on the floor and beg for more "kiss, kiss."

But all in all, have fun.

7

Service Oriented Stuff (S.O.S)

Isn't it good that people are different? Imagine a world where everyone was just like us. The horror. Picture a world where everyone eats sail-fish and yogurt sandwiches and like to listen to Porky Pig tapes backwards seeking subliminal messages. But also of note: if everyone was the same, who would be providing the services we so necessarily need? Even those moguls of the corporate world need their cars repaired, their garbage taken out and their clothes cleaned. If it wasn't for service oriented individuals CEOs would be going to work in clothes so smelly they make noise, and in cars so beat up they only work downhill. In other words, we all need service-oriented businesses. But because of that need many of these establishments are swamped with CEOs. How can you as a business owner lessen your popularity? We will look at a number of service-based establishments along with additional professions that fill a need and list a few of the top anti-success methods for your benefit:

COMPUTER CONSULTANT

The technology field has been growing in leaps and bounds within these past few years. Because of the rise of, among other things, "no wires needed" network servers and EZ-Pass brain implants, there's an ever-growing need for administrators, programmers and consultants. Without these fields filled a company's growth is severely hindered. But what about you? You may be in this field. You may be one of those people who are on call 24 hours a day, 7 days a week. You picked the computer consultant field because you wanted to control your time and your schedule, but now it's controlling you.

At first, being paged worked like a charm. Initially you got your pages at the right time: like the time your next door neighbor wanted to show you his baby's pictures for the third time that week ("See how much she's grown since Wednesday?"), or that time when you said the customary "how ya doing?" to your mailman and *he actually started to tell you.* At those times your pager went off, you apologized and left enthusiastically. But now it's getting crazy. The pages have now stopped you from enjoying life and have caused you to miss some very important events: You missed the ending of the Women's Crochet League's annual Speed-Crochet Tournament, you missed the ending of the groundbreaking Disney/CNN collaboration: "When Caricatures Attack," and you missed who Oprah Winfrey's guest vegetarian whisperer was. How can you fail in this vast field and regain your life?

The "Oops!" Method—Where did this beautiful word ever come from? This word has come to signify the error of man, the imperfection of humanity as he goes on day to day in life. This word naturally comes out when an individual has taken an action or made a statement that was unexpected or/and has caused an unexpected booboo. Like the time you were on line to see the sequel to Titanic, "Iceberg On The Run," and struck up a conversation with the pregnant woman behind you. You asked her if she was expecting triplets, but *he* wasn't. "Oops." In other words it's another way of saying, with a pat on the victim's back "Hey, I'm only human." But for those who are looking to fail in the computer field, it is a word among words (wordamunxious) because it enables the errorer to walk away scot-free (and free from more work) by in essence saying, "Hey, I'm only human-bye!" And it can clean up the most irritating of actions…especially when followed by these choice phrases:

"…you hired me to work?"

"…I wasn't hiding. I thought this would be a good place for a er, um, wire thingy."

"…I thought that was the 'de-light' key. It was kind of dark in here."

"…you wanted the printer hooked up? I thought you wanted the water cooler server online."

"…so you didn't want your diary made accessible?"

"…I thought you *wanted* the boss to know your score."

"…so you don't use Turtle Basic here?"

"…I always carry a joystick around with me."

"…so you didn't want those pictures circulated?"

"…so that wasn't your sister's picture I installed on the corporate screen saver?"

"…I thought you told me that "Mr. Toupee" was your boss' real name. I think he wants to talk to you."

So use the "oops" and you will find it's an easy way to the peaceful life. Soon there would be no more unwanted pages, beeps and blips. Soon there would be no more emergencies and computer virus attacks. Use the free time and see what's on Oprah.

CATERING

The festive evening. Isn't it so memorable when we are invited to a catered affair. Chances are the host thought it better to cater than to ask their friends and relatives to provide the food. And this makes sense. Would your company really want to savor Aunt Martha's Milk and Lemon Juice Shake or Uncle Wobblinski's Vinegar-Baking Soda eggnog?

Of course not. So professionalism reigns supreme. But how can you, as a caterer make these affairs to remember?

- "Catch Your Own Chicken Day"

This age old custom is a source of fun and enjoyment for all. After hors d'oeuvre are served announce that there will be a little twist for dinner

and allow 15 chickens to run wild. Don't worry if there is initially horror and shock, someone will jump into the fray and catch their meals.
Like your mother used to say: "If they want to eat, they'll eat even if
they have to chase the meat."

• Dietizers

Americans are fat. That is what the latest surveys are saying. Americans
are on the top of the heap in average overweightness. But it shouldn't
surprise anyone. Look at all the fast food stores, fast food commercials
and fast food professionals out there. So how can you do your part to
keep your part of the United States from sinking below sea level?
Dietizers. These nifty snackies are appetizers that are great for pushing,
scaring and even starving the fat away from your guests. Here is one
scrumptious example:

CLEAVON BRITTLES

1 bag of truffles (12)

2 gallons Tofu fritters

16oz container of beet juice

2 larger castor fruits (diced)

¼ teaspoon sugar

10 cups water

2 cups tabasco sauce

½ cup wheat germ

4 cups whole bran flour

6 gallons vegetable oil

DIRECTIONS: Take the flour and mix with necessary amounts of water until dough forms. Divide dough into six round sections. Knead each section exactly 207 times (no more) and flatten. Mix tofu, castor fruit and Tabasco sauce into a gel and put on top of three of the dough patties. Put four truffles on each tofu concoction and cover with remaining dough patties. But be mindful to squeeze the ends so that the tofu doesn't slip out during the cooking process and attack. When done let sit for three days and then put in oven at 350 degrees. Let cook for 30 minutes and take out when brown (or when an audible moan sounds). Cut into bite sized pieces (feeds 250).

The wheat germs can be used as an additional appetizer by putting each wheat germ kernel on a toothpick and laying them attractively on a tissue. Vegetable oil can be used on the ground around the appetizer table to provide a rip-slipping calorie burning ordeal to get the eatings.

So, do well in your catering assignment and happy exiting!

DAY CARE SERVICE

The life of a parent has its rewards, but also its pressures. Along with the daily chores and employment, there's also the responsibility of taking care of a child that they need to think of. At times, though, these two responsibilities clash. Who is there to pick up the slack? The Day Care Service provider. Trusted professionals whose aim is to provide a haven for the child while the parents take care of other pressing responsibilities. But what can a Day Care Service provider do to fail in this practice and free themselves to experience life's abounding pleasures? Here are some nice suggestions:

• Oatmeal Fight Day
It has long been known that oatmeal has medicinal qualities. Its healing oats have been used to heal stress, mosquito bites and the like. Show the young ones under your care how to make it in a pot (adult supervision), let it cool and let the house have it! Who knows, probably oatmeal's medicinal qualities extend to wallpaper, leather sofas, porce-

lain and drop ceilings. This is also an opportunity for children to learn the age-old children's game, "Hide The Oatmeal," and the fine art of house cleaning.

• Draw Mommy When She Wakes Up
Art is one of the oldest forms of expression. By means of art individuals have been able to illustrate their feelings, draw their joys and fears. Teach these tots to draw what is close to them: their Mommy in the morning. Imagine the fear some children have when Mommy wakes them up in her make-up less, coifed-less, drool-ridden glory. This could be mentally damaging to the child. But by putting their fears to paper it can help the child see that with a little crayon, the world could be a happier place. One of the 500 copies can be given to the Mother as a reminder of the joy of small things while the rest can be passed out in the neighborhood.

• Tape Mommy And Daddy Fighting
Technology. To think, before the advent of television and radio our lives centered around our own little community which felt like it was the whole world to us. But now, inventions have shaped and groomed mankind in ways that would have seemed like impossibilities years ago.

Unlike children from yonder years, children today are in tune with technology. From pre-K they are in touch with computers, electronic toys, beepers and the like. Children can thus use these "tech toys" to play and learn at the same time. As a Day Care provider, teach the kids under your direction the fine art of Conversation Taping using a popular "tech toy," the mini-tape recorder. Their first project can be taping Mommy and Daddy arguing. By taping these conversations, children learn sentence structure, nicknames, human weaknesses, strengths, the art of persuasion and most of all, what Mommy and Daddy do with their money. After everyone in your class has gotten their taped arguments, you can compare them, award a winner and put these eye-opening sound bites highlighting the beauty and complexity of homosapien communication on the internet for all to hear. Start this up and you'll be helping your responsibilities ready themselves for new things to come (including marriage).

• Scream like a pro lessons

In the Day Care field the responsible adult has to deal with the ways of a child; their crying, their stubbornness, even their screaming. While the crying and the stubbornness is a regular aspect of childhood, the screaming can be molded into a fine musical tone that works best with proper training at high decibels. Imagine the fun when children learn to scream Mommy's name in three different octaves. Imagine the fun the child will have waking Mommy and Daddy up or making Mommy and Daddy jump at the breakfast table. Teach them the finer art of screaming; when, where and how long. Advanced lessons will help the tot scream their favorite tune. And with multilingual studies being a popular class in school, show them how to yell "Fire!" in German, French and the guttural slang of the Mid-Plains Thurgs. Fun is around the corner.

• Teach all the laws (tax, traffic, marriage)

Isn't it wonderful when children are brought up to be honest, law abiding citizens? That is one thing this world needs more of: more honest, law abiding individuals still enjoying their first set of teeth. Some want to wait until the child is older before teaching these finer points of the legal establishment, but the best time to groom them is now. Not only is this a benefit to the child as he grows up in this world that is increasingly unlawabiding, but the child can also help parents who have swayed in their honest law abiding mentality. Make sure that the children under your care say these reminders nicely, respectably and LOUDLY in order to successfully spark remembrance of the civil law:

TRAFFIC LAWS

"Mommy? Wasn't that a dead like Fred red light?"
"Daddy? What did you call that traffic officer? He didn't hear you."
"Daddy? Is that your car that you are rifling through?

"Mommy? Isn't 105 more than 55?"

"Daddy? Didn't that old man get to this parking spot first?

PERSONAL PROPERTY LAW

"Grandma, did you pay for that grape?"

"Daddy? I counted sixteen food stuff-isn't that too much for this line?"

"Daddy? Why are we speeding away from that car we just hit?"

MISCELLANEOUS

"Daddy? Doesn't that tip belong to that other table?"

"Mommy? How did you pass inspection with a broken headlight?"

"Mommy that spit didn't go in the garbage."

"Daddy. I just told the nice man at the door that you said you weren't home. He wants to speak to you. How did he know you were home?"

SPEECH

Human speech has always been a fascination to mankind. From the simplest of tongues to languages that are almost impossible to learn, speech has played a major part in mankind's growth and continuation in this worldwide specter. Modern pediatricians have noted that parents should not try to lower their level and speak "baby talk" to their children. This is not advisable in that it hampers personal growth and mental maturity—not to mention the affect it will also have on the children. So parents are to speak to their child as they speak to anyone else. But as a Day Care provider you can help the children enlarge their vocabulary by teaching them to respond to their parents in these upstanding ways:

 * Instead of saying "yes"-have them say, with eyes almost closed, eyebrows raised and chin tilted up slightly, "indubitably."

* Refer to all facial blemishes as "ichthyosis."
* Say, "By George I thinks you's got it."

- Like Father like Son

The bond between a Father and son cannot be relinquished. Teach the children to be just like their dad. How? Teach them to imitate their father in everything the father does. Everything. Cement that bond. When the Father tires out or tries to lose the son in a crowd, teach the son to fight for that bond-cry! In no time the father would be back to continue the training.

- Grammar correction

Doesn't it bother you to hear someone speak bad English. We're not talking about those that just came to the country (they could learn the language by taking up the customer service field—see chapter 1). We're talking about those that know the language but mercilessly, without regard, fribbilate it to pieces. Teach the children under your care to pick up on bad lingo and correct it, bringing fine sounding pronunciations, correct pace and pitch into the air. After the lessons children would be helping their parents in a fine way. And once again these should be said respectfully and LOUD:

> "Mommy, you used that word wrong."
> "Daddy, &%$@#$ is not in the dictionary."
> "Mommy, that sentence is missing a past participle."
> "Daddy, 'Go!' is not a full sentence."

- Health Alerters

Americans are not very healthy. Why? The media, through advertising, has bombarded us with the need for this and the need for that causing a wave of people to eat new things that aren't good for them. Parents are continually looking for second, third and fourth medical opinions. But what if the children were taught proper health elements and knew how to spot bad medical symptoms? This would be a boon to the parents as their young ones could notice from afar areas where the parents can adjust and *without charge* let the parents know:

"Mommy? You have too many fat cells"
"Daddy? Can you see your toes?"
"Mommy, plastic surgery can hide those chins"
"Mommy, that makeup can't hide the ichthyosis."
"Mommy, are you supposed to wheeze when you put those jeans on?"
"Daddy? You didn't wash your hands after using the bathroom."

• One-two-three

One of the earliest forms of education a child is given is the ability to count. Ancient Cyberterians were known for their counting skills. Ancient cuneiform showed that the young men in this tribe, on their path into manhood were commanded to balance on their big toe while counting the arrows shot into the air. Just on a side note, after much research we believe that the Toe God statue, Fungisapel that was unearthed in Monte Cristo in 1937 was the god of these ancient counters. But of course that is our theory. We will, as usual, wait for the world to catch up. But in any case, why not teach the child under your care to count everything? Imagine the wealth of wisdom and insight this child will accumulate in no time:

"Daddy, that is the eighth beer you've had."
"Mommy. That will make 5,678 calories for today."
"Daddy, how come the telephone bill has 20 900 numbers?"
"Daddy, is that $10 you are taking out of Mommy's purse?
"Mommy? You've said 'leave me alone' thirty-eight times."

And you can even teach these ditties:

• Count to 5 million class (ages 2-6)
    "…four million nine hundred and twenty thousand and six bottles of beer on the wall…" (for long car trips)

- Stocks and Bonds surmisation course

- Smell distinguishing

Kids. According to one unsubstantiated rumor, we were kids once. We so much treasure the time and energy and money our parents put into us as they worked with us, put up with us and groomed us for our journey into adulthood. Thanks to their loving hands we were prepared to take on the responsibilities of work, obnoxious workmates, paying taxes, shelling out money every month to keep our cars running, losing quarters in that dumb machine whenever we tried to wash our clothes…living from check to check…hmmmm…Mom? Dad? Can we come back home?

PET CARE

What to do with Fido? This is an ever-present question that comes up every vacation time, every family crisis and every allergic relative's visit. Of course they call you and of course you take on the feline/canine responsibility. But what can you do to stop them from coming back to you when they're in need of pet sitting?

• "The" training
Have their dog jump around and bark wildly each time the word "the" is spoken. Impressive.

• Fetch the Police
Wouldn't it be a nice gesture if a police officer was around at all times to provide security for your family? Pet care specialists can teach the dogs under their care to find a cop and bring him to his master's house for no reason at all at any time at all. Of course, the cop wouldn't like it but how often does one get a chance to greet one of their fellow community protectors at 3:18 a.m.? Got a doughnut?

• "Oops!"
Wouldn't it be funny if your dog faints when you kiss it? Of course not

(at least not to the owner). But dog's have an acute sense of smell that is rarely used. Train the dogs in your care to whine, run around in circles, point and faint at the scent of bad breath. This helps the dog to provide a fine service for his master.

Pets. You gotta love them, but better yet, let their owners do the loving. With these good suggestions you'll be going dogless in no time (or catless for you cat lovers out there). Sigh.

WEDDING CONSULTANT

As a wedding consultant you have a career that can add to the happiness of two people. Even though the focus is on them, that is, their marriage, the wedding is a privilege bestowed upon invited guests. You have the assignment of making this day unforgettable. We fondly remember a former workmate, Guy Fuymenstien, who married a very nice girl. He was twenty and she was forty-seven. He was 124 lbs., she was 276 lbs. They always said that destiny loved the number 400 (their combined weight) and they did their best to stay at that romantic number. Of course, over the years their romantic number increased, but the love did likewise. She was the best girl for him. Why do we say so? She was always there to pick him up. It was so romantic seeing them playing horseback in the park. When he sat on her shoulders his face lit up like he was on top of the world. And he so loved to be on her shoulders. From time to time he would bend down and give her a wet upside down kiss. We get glossy eyed just thinking about it.

But it was their wedding that blew us away. It was big, beautiful extravagant and cheap. The plastic utensils and the cake were rented. They met their best man an hour before the wedding as he was getting ready for another wedding that evening on the floor below. The photographer only took two shots (panoramic, of course) and the music was from Minnie Drydells Kindergarten Kazoo class. But it was love. When the justice of the peace gave the okay for the bride to pick up the groom and kiss, we almost didn't watch. Sigh. That's how weddings should be. They will have their problems, but, sigh, you got to love them. But of course, you don't want to succeed as a wedding consultant. So, add some spice to this affair and, lo and behold, never be called again!

You can always put the scare in couples when the topic of spending comes up. Though there's business at any price, whether they say "budget" or "sky's the limit" you must be ready to provide some of these surprise features:

- Limousine (stretch '80 Pacer Sedan)

- Music: Tape of your Karaoke sessions (mixed by DJ Press Play)

- Invitations sent COD

- Paper/Corduroy tuxedos

- Hefty Plastic Wedding Dress (sandwich bag veil—preferably 3-ply)

Everyone loves surprises. If those video cameras are ready there will be hours of fun and fond remembrance after this evening. Here are some surprise options that can be implemented on the wedding day. But of course, the happy couple does not need to know what you will add, or when it will be implemented. Happy planning!

- Make the wedding cake people look EXACTLY like the couple (e.g. down to the triple chin)

- Cake surprises
  Sushi
  Rented Cakes ("Don't touch!" written in icing)
  Tofu Frosting/Filling
  Wax Cakes

- Surprise Guests

Sometimes there is a tendency to forget those ones who have affected our lives in so many unmentionable ways. And, chances are, the bride and groom in all their running around to get their wedding together, forgot about those very ones. Wouldn't it be a touching surprise to bring these ones in to give a speech?

Old girlfriends/boyfriends
Creditors
Bounty Hunter
The Peepee Boy
Bill collectors
Stiffed Waiters
Parole Officer
Stiffed Bookies
Psychologists
The Masked Stalker

• Paid criers

Who's not touched by the joining of two? Most are. But what if nobody is touched? Paid criers always add impact and sensitivity to a marriage ceremony. They come in a variety of levels:

Light   -sniffle

Medium   -cry, wail, drool

Heavy   -pull out hair, bawl, contort ("Attack Groom" option)

• Old lady security

There will be no purloining of wedding gifts at this feast. These unfeisty security pillars will go to each table, to each person during the course of the day to make sure they maintain honesty to the nth degree. They can also be called upon to follow the bride all day and ALL night.

AUTO REPAIR

Betsy, your car, is like a faithful pet. There for you in good times and bad. But there are times, like pets, when Betsy needs that boost. Probably the years have taken a toll on her body work, or the daily grind of life has weakened her inner parts, or that 54 octane "just like gas" special from Booboo's Gas and Tummy Tucks did a "special" on her engine. But that is where the ubiquitous auto repairman comes to play. With a head full of knowledge and a hand full of grease he can take Besty into his caring arms and nurse her back to purring health. But if he does this, too much word of mouth can spell his doom! Before he knows it more and more cars will be parading in. Before he knows it more and more referred relatives of past clients will "buddy" him for a discount. How can he slow down this onslaught?

- Too much air in one tire

- Hire Original New York squeegees (tourists would love it)

- Serve cold coffee and tofu bagels with horseradish center

- Let each blow of the horn trigger the driver's side "Squeeze-Me" cushion

- "Mouse in Car" joke

- Antialignment

- Tow the car away joke

BRING IT TO THE STREET!

The street fair/expo is a fine place to go to showcase your art, services or fashions. Walking money bags lurk on shady streets looking for the next best thing, the next big deal. Don't let it be you! Many have been "found" at these shows and went on to nauseous success, forgetting about their families and stressing themselves out looking for another concept. But here are some booth concepts that will not be a hit at the latest expositor event:

Prelicked Cuties

Start Up Cost: $1,700

A licked candy is the ultimate craft to start. Finding bags of candy is easy (or try www.prelickedcandy.com for those that don't want to do any licking) and after a good messy lick you just attach paper hands and feet (no need for glue!). A ball of hair from your local barber shop can top it off (and provide a mustache or two). Have fun!

BB Boys

Start up Cost: $575

Belly button lint is a little known means of revitalizing an ancient craft. In Ancient Pagmolia (deep in the jungles of ancient Nevada) the Pagmolians saved up months of belly button lint (*muck-shefem*) and made tribal wear for their annual inter-tribal battles/proms. This went on for centuries until one tribe found this aspect rather tasteless and felt there was a slight chance that this tradition may hold them back from being accepted into modern society (and thusly a stint on National Geographic).

You can revitalize this tradition by following ancient preset patterns to make BB Boys. These lively dolls are 100% natural (unless you collect artificial lint) and are loads of fun. It may help to separate the different lint donations by name in case, for example, you find that different colors have a greater or lesser dexterity which may affect the use and aesthetic appeal of your BB Boys.

Whole Foods Cracker Repair Booth

Start up Cost: $34,000

Have you ever bought a bag of crackers from your favorite corner store only to find that some of the crackers, especially the bottom ones, were cracked? Didn't that get you upset? (If it did you would like our upcoming title: "Get a Life!") But in any case, the handy dandy cracker repairman is always ready to handle this delicate case. By using all natural adhesives, he can repair the cracker to perfection so that it goes into their mouths and tea and under their cheese the right way, whole.

Regular Joe Autograph Signing

Starting Up cost: $25,100.01

Your Uncle Phil was a very good wrought iron maintainer. For thirty years he molded and maintained wrought iron fences around the county. But ever since his retirement, it's been years since he's twisted any wrought iron into the works of art that they were. What would give him a boost? Have him sign autographs in your traveling Regular Joe's Autograph Signing Tour. There are hordes of wrought iron fence maintainer groupies around. We think that Uncle Phil would love the attention. But it doesn't have to stop there. Your neighbor found a 1989 penny, have him do some signing. What about your best friend's second cousin Bertha? Her signature would be priceless. Didn't she once meet someone who knew somebody that saw someone who was actually in the studio audience of the Chevy Chase talk show? Bring them along!

SECURITY

Oofalla didn't choose the security field because he liked it. It was a field that sort of came to him. Even from small, when individuals saw his amazing girth, they automatically gave him security work; from pamper patrol to the pee pee posse. He didn't mind at that young age since the money (large shiny coins) was good. But as he got older his fame spread (as did his collar size). Movie stars and the like wanted him bad. They called him the "Security Czar," "the Movie Star's Moose" and a whole bunch of assorted nicknames that irked him. But what eventually happened? Oofalla lost his mind and is currently serving time for celebrity liposuction theft. We're sorry we had to put a pause to the niceties to this point and touch on such a serious topic. But it has to be said. With bloodshot eyes and quivering lips we say: "Don't let success ruin you or your new denim sneakers!" It's not worth it. If you find that you're being haggled and pushed and poked into the security field this book is for you. If you find that you're being swamped every day to protect another four-foot celebrity read this carefully. We want you to fail in style. But how does one fail in style in an area where clients' lives are at stake? Read on and be AMAZED.

The Flex—As a bodyguard you know that your clients love to get media attention. They say that they don't, but if they didn't why'd they volunteer to show their new tattoo on a 15 x 25 foot screen to paying customers—eating *popcorn* at that (which has been well documented to enhance visual receptors)? So, since they want attention, be their attention-getter! Flex. Next time you're walking them across a busy city street—flex! Show the muscles that made you a security provider to the stars. Of course, be polite and tell those under your care to wait so you don't lose them, but by all means, flex to your heart's content! And just to add pizzazz wear a "Joe's Rent-a-Muscle" tattoo (removable).

Advertise—As a security miester your many other talents are probably forgotten—DO NOT LET YOUR TALENTS DIE. A survey of 356 security/bodyguards revealed something interesting: 5% threw the surveyor out of a moving car, 18% yelled a spittle-drenched "What are you doing in here?", 24% slept with teddy bears and a whopping 54% wanted to be in Public Relations! (+/-64%). So, speak up! Make sure your clients' names stay in the paper for longer than fifteen minutes! How? Whenever a cameraman or a reporter appears while you're protecting your clients, serve them these patented ditties:

> "I'm sorry. No pictures. The flash bulbs may wrinkle their just completed plastic surgery."

> "Could you please refrain from questions? My clients are still doing their 'How to Pass a Lie Detector Test' home correspondence course."

"Could you stay away from my client? Only I have the chemical attack training to take the stench of their putrid body odor."

"I'm taking a break. You can chase and harass my clients for only a half hour."

"Could you please leave my client alone and let them dispose of the missing body in peace?"

In no time you would be free from the paparazzi's morbid persistence, free from the ego bursts of your clients and you'll even be able to smile in public for the first time. Good fortune to you.

REPORTER

But let's look at the other side of the microphone. Top notch reporters are seen as the most trustworthy people on the face of the planet. By their presenting of local news and world events they've surpassed second grade teachers to top the respect earners list. But this also adds to the stress in their lives, especially if they're famous. Everywhere they go it's, (mouth agape) "Want a story? I just had my tonsils taken out" or, "What's the average amount of time people lose their place while eating cereal?" or the dreaded, "Do you see me when you're looking at the camera?" At times it takes other extremes: (whispered) "Don't talk so loud. Mr. Reporter will hear you and tell the whole world about that molar," or, "I heard you wear Barney boxers below the camera." The horror.

This staff has researched in great detail what you as a reporter has to go through. We KNOW that you're not a walking encyclopedia. We know that you're not a blabbermouth. We know that you don't want to know about every story. We're still working on the Barney boxer rumor, but that should be clarified in time. So how do you evade the rambunctious questionings and false reasonings? Give the audience what they want. Reporters LOVE those rare, unscripted opportunities at interviews where they can ask any question they wish. Use this opportunity to get to the meat of the story. Your viewers will giggle

with glee (but we can't say the same about your station heads). Listen
to this fine performance by ex-reporter Travis McGweel:

> "So, Morbid—"
> "For the twelfth time, it's 'Mary!'"
> "Sorry—Minerva. Minerva, did you really sing on your last
> album?"
> "Of course I did. You heard it."
> "Oh. That was you? And I thought it was my CD playing back-
> wards."
> "Why you—"
> "My apologies. But as a reporter I have to be frank…(singing)
> Strangers in the night…."
> "What are you doing?"
> "Being frank. Frank Sinatra. You recognize the voice?"
> "No. But I recognize the words. At least that survived."
> "So you *did* have an affair with Frank."
> "Of course not. I never met the guy?"
> (To staff) "Can you bring out that package?"

The staff brings out a plastic wrapper.

> "What's that?"
> "A wrapper that was found in your house."
> "What does a chicken wrapper have to do with anything?"
> "You said you didn't have an affair with Frank and the proof is
> here!"
> "A chicken wrapper?"
> "Not just any chicken wrapper. Frank's."
> "Frank's?"
> "Frank Perdue. The Chicken Czar! (standing on chair) Long may
> he live!"

Police come out and wrestle handcuffs onto Minerva, er, uh, Mary.
This excerpt showed the creative way Travis mixed deep, thought provoking questions with an inquisition—just the right balance to lose his
job. There are other ways that aren't as subtle:

- Whenever you get a late breaking story (male reporters) pull off your clip on tie, and rip your shirt with gusto (two hands) from the collar while yelling, "By the gods!"

- When interviewing individuals hold microphone up to their ears.

- Unbeknownst to your reluctant, fleeing interviewee attach a lie detector with Shock Sensor® to them and ask away (good television)!

- Stare into the screen and eerily say, "I see you."

With these proven methods you won't be called on an assignment for a while. You'll be free to bask in your peace of mind. Now, about those Barney boxers…

HEADHUNTERS

Headhunters are in such a need these days. Especially in the technology field. In New York alone there are 300,000 tech jobs going unfilled this year. It's the job of the Headhunter to find the right person for the job. But what if you goofed? What if you found a person that was so well suited for the job you found for them their DNA matched the tile deposits located on the company's conference room floor? So right that when they met the CEO for the first time, their suit matched the CEO's wallpaper. They even had a natural beauty mark that, when looked at in the right light, was a spitting three-dimensional image of the company's corporate logo. EVERYONE is going to want you to headhunt for them. You're now receiving calls after calls after calls to headhunt. What to do?

Here are some award winning responses to those numerous requests:

> "An accountant? No. No accountants on my roster, but I have a counting horse that owes me a favor—"

"Didn't I just send you a gopher last week? Oh. So you didn't want the rodent you wanted the other kind."

"No. I don't have any junior executive secretaries on my list, but I do have a whole box of sea slug parfait—the low calorie variety."

"Yes. I sent him. Yeah, I know he's wearing his shoes backwards. Yeah, I know he's mumbling to himself—Yeah, I know he likes to belt out off-broadway tunes off tune. Why I sent him? You said you needed a hand. He has two! What are you looking for? A Martian?"

Headhunters. You gotta love 'em. But they need to enjoy life also, right?

MODELS

Walk that walk. Talk that—sorry, don't talk. That's the model's life for you. But for what they do they get PAID. But most models will tell you, off camera, that they're not happy with the lavish, gluttonously wealthy lifestyle they live. They'll tell you about all the jealousy, backbiting and dishonesty that goes on—and that's just their plumbers! Imagine everyone else. Germaldine DeFloosh a former model, knew that life style oh too well. Her face has appeared on everything from Vague magazine to the bulletin board in the post office on the corner of Ninth and Madison. We have a recording of her interview with reporter Xavier Reivax a not-so-upcoming news reporter. In this taped interview, that we went to great pains to print, we see the pains, pressures and internal coofimations that Ms. DeFloosh faced as a runway model:

Xavier:	Ms. DeFloosh. It's been known that the life of a model is an outwardly glamorous but inwardly sad life.
Defloosh:	Yes. Nobody listens to—

Xavier:	Would you say that many people need to hear from someone that's been there about the perils that they face? Do you think that by the public learning about this they can even moreso feel for these misunderstood divas?
Defloosh:	Y-yeah. I feel that—
Xavier:	True. True. Well said. I, myself, after listening to you have changed my mind about models. I used to think they were shallow, two-faced, selfish and had a strange affinity to mango seeds. But after talking with you and by your opening up to me, I see that you don't even like mangoes and that the vast majority of the 104 in our nationwide listening audience have been wrong.
Defloosh:	I didn't—
Xavier:	That will be all. Thank you, and good night.

Ms. Defloosh took the "How to Fail" home correspondence course and went from the bright lights to bar room fights. No more annoying shoots. She's finally eating how and what she wants. No more ice cube sandwiches and tofu shakes for her! Here are some nifty ideas she successfully took to heart to regain her peace of mind:

- The next time you're called to do a shoot wear a fake leg under your dress and yell, "Okay! Who did this?"

- When going out to eat, eat like a pig and ask the maitre'd to bring you your fifth and sixth servings first.

- Always show up in public in a loving cuddle with an escaped convict.

- Whenever they're putting your makeup on pretend that the force of the lipstick is so strong that it sends you reeling out the chair, unto the floor and rolling up the steps (instant Emmy!).

- Groom your underarm hair (ladies) to be between 3" and 4" long. If you are UHD (underarm-hair-deficient) get extensions. Once they've grown make it a point when in public to wear a tank top with a collar and wave, wave, wave!

- When posing with adoring male fans give them Class III wedgies (the strongest wedgies that can legally be administered in New York and its surrounding towns. If you're not in New York, check with the authorities first). Use your 2 ½ foot height advantage to the fullest!

- Don't let the arm lock by your security and the head lock by your agent stop you from chasing open mikes! Give an interview! Let the world see that behind that beautiful face is a woman with a severe, spittle-spewing lisp with something to say!

HELP HELP

What a wonderful world we live in. A world where opportunity is around the corner. A place where, no matter what your background is, you can make it. There was this one guy on 42nd street in New York with the most creative money making technique we've ever seen. He dressed himself in all gold, down to the painted face and hands. He stood still like a mannequin on a box while holding a cup. In front of him was a bucket that was filled with cash and coins. Where did he get the money from? Curious tourists and bored New Yorkers would put money in his cup—and then the show would begin! He would lift up one hand and then put it down and lift up the other hand and put it down (which dropped the money into his bucket) while he tooted with a whistle in his mouth. That was it. Your coins (or dollars) were gone after two seconds—then he was still like a statue again. To think.

Those days we could've used some extra money this idea never came to mind!

But this country has another edge to it that makes it unique. People with problems have a place to go for help. And to make it easier for them to remember, it's abbreviated: AAAA, MAD, etc. But what has come of this? These establishments are swamped with people! Newspaper and television coverage has broadcasted their healing abilities worldwide. What if you're a CEO of a successful SAE (Successful Abbreviated Establishment) that, pardon the rapidly approaching all-caps, WANTS HIS LIFE BACK? What can you do? Change your reach. There are a number of people out there whose problems, weaknesses, addictions and goals aren't cared for. Target these groups. We have a number of them to follow. They can use an experienced "big cheese." In no time you'll be "ahhhh—ing" to the sounds of peace as hustle and bustle slowly melts away.

ATR—The Association for Three-Ply Reform—This company champions the use of three-ply sandwich bags.

BBLI—Belly Button Lint Investigators. This nifty group follows any belly button lint theft complaints on the East coast (also seeking West coast rep).

AST—Association for Samurai Twins. This group is trying to push legislation that enables more samurai **twins** be used in general market advertising.

TKA—The Tree Kickers Association is the most ingenious of this list. Their job is to kick trees so hard that all the leaves come down saving customers the task of daily raking the leaves in the fall season. They seek a representative who'll take them seriously (and give great toe massages).

TRW—The Traveling Rap Whistlers. This musical group whistles popular rap tunes and is looking for a manager to promote tours and book signings for them.

OCV—Organization for the Chronically Vague—They do something, but we're not too sure.

KGSG—Kindergartners with Goatees Support Group. This group stands up for these long haired tykes. The KGSG also needs someone to help them raise money to research this phenom and help them in promoting their vanilla pudding/aftershave concoction.

PDWA—The Paint Drying Watchers Association. This organization is growing rapidly and may not be in the next issue of this publication—too much success! But in the meantime, they can use a leader.

ABFGFC—The Association for Battery Free Gas Free Cars. This group is the boldest of all the groups listed. They are looking for someone who can stand up to the gas and electric industry. Their proposal is to save the world from energy waste, battery disposal and toxic fumes by creating extension cords for cars that plug into the car owner's homes. These extension cords will be retractable by just a push of a button located on the car's steering wheel. The cords length will vary: from the Corner Store length (200ft) to the Cross Country Traveler length (185,000 ft). Over the years they've quickened the speed of the retractabalizer from five hours to 2 hours.

So. CEOs, tell the wife (your latest one) and the kids (if they remember you) that you're going to spend more time with them than ever before! Ignore the sour faces they make and have fun!

MARRIAGE COUNSELORS

Dr. Eg Yudonwanano knows full well the stress that comes from successfully saving marriages. We weren't able to get a direct quote from this marriage healer because of his ongoing alimony proceedings, but he needed to fail—badly. His own marriage became rocky when his book, entitled, "Put The 'H' Back in Marriage" became a runaway best-seller helping pot-throwing, dish-dodging, money-complaining couples to unite. EVERYONE and their mother now wanted marital advice from him after this book. Soon he was here and there and here again, but his family never saw him. The dog bit him twice (and this was after the dog read his name tag!) and the city's last remaining towncrier made a citizen's arrest when he saw the good doctor entering *his own house* at three in the morning. What to do? Here is some choice advice we sent Doctor Eg that he can implement after the hearings:

- When a feuding husband and wife enters the office have your secretary wheel out your new 689 page pre-application form.

- Couples should be one, shouldn't they? Why not add the Siamese Solution to your list of marital aid options? This method incorporates the unique Siamese twins concept whereby through 16 hour surgery the husband and the wife get attached at the hip. Romantic.

- As the first client of the day enters, fake a fight between your wife and yourself. Fake blood should do the trick.

- Interview problem couples while sitting on your wife's lap dressed only in diapers (quilted preferably).

- Break into convulsions, congested spitting sessions, drooling-spattering-stuttering episodes whenever you have to mention the words "marriage," or "married."

Hopefully with these ideas active, Dr. Yudonwanano can attain the peace that he cherishes. The doctor once made a very profound statement at the annual, "Nothing Else to Do But Listen to Doctors Rant" seminar. He said, "The biggest cause of divorce is marriage." Deep. As we write this we're still immobile in our seats with awestruckedness. After leaving that seminar, Bookster, one of our temps, was motivated even moreso to stay single until he got married. No ifs, ands or buts. But (oops!) if (oops again!) a free Saturday came along, he just may take the leap.

AUTOMOBILE DESIGNER

Richard looks at the television and shakes his head so vigorously that his dentures continue rattling for minutes after he stops. Years ago Richard was in the same position that the young man on the screen was. The young man on the television show, "We Want to Know What You Know, You Know?" was the designer of the soon to be cult classic the Chrysler PT Bruiser.

"Poor guy. He thinks it's going to be horseradish and peaches, but he has a world of problems around the corner."

Richard would know. Years earlier, in 1960, he was the mastermind behind the Clutch sports car. When that car came off the assembly line you couldn't help but run to it (or *away* from it depending on who's driving). It had 22 inch rims and a monster under the hood. Once his creation came onto the car scene it was nothing but party after party after party for Richard. But how did he feel at the end of the day? "Like a near-sighted Peruvian rhino that forgot where it left its booko-booko berries."

Okay…

"Before my design took off nobody noticed me. It was great. Nobody invited me to the company picnics. I showed up anyway and they made me bob for lobsters and made me play 'find the apple in the hornet's nest.' They always made *me* the piñata. I missed those days. My pursuit of the finer things in life has amounted to nothing. Give me the good old days! Give me the cheerful times once again!"

We had to wrestle Richard to the floor. But you see what success did to him? How can a future automobile designer ward off this onslaught?

• In your next car creation program the car to note any increased weight of the driver:

"Sarah. You're 22 lbs more than yesterday."

- Because of the prevalence of sleep depraved drivers on the road there are a number of gizmos that can alert a sleeping driver that he's nodding and needs to take few minutes or hours of sleep by the side of the road. But why wait till then? Install a mechanism that squirts water into the face of the driver every time he *blinks.*

- Most people wouldn't tell you this, but they hate their car roofs. The reason why there is no national outcry nor attempted coups is because there is never a roof design option—they had no choice. The answer? Drop ceilings! And to top it off, a 3-foot roof fan.

CAR SECURITY

Criminals are out there. They're looking for every opportunity to sneak a wallet, pilfer a Snickers bar and even steal your car. These criminals will take it like it's a three-sided dollar. How do we thwart these wheel-lubbers while at the same time fail as a car designer?

RemomboLock—This new car door handle combination lock is the answer. But isn't it hard to remember numbers at times? Yes it is. We've all been given telephone numbers to remember and before we knew it, forgot it (because none of the numbers were related). But as a former workmate of our office for 30 years said (We can't remember his name as of this writing), our brains were just lacking the exercise needed to remember things properly. The same with car owners. The average door handle lock is not made in a way to train the mind. RememboLock is. It sets the car to automatically change the combination at random times. It could be 2-2-5-7 one minute and then after lunch 5-0-9-8, and 2-2-2-8-9-4 every third Saturday and the Sunday that follows it, but, of course, every other week. The numbers will also change depending on the climate and where the car is located. How will the car owner know which number is when and where? A 1,500 page chart will keep them up to par! But don't let this chart get into the hands of those criminals. Safe parking!

Flexo Lock—This will be the other lock option on the next big car. Will "Stretch" Willy, a former contortionist and Twister champion has designed a lock that is both practical and health oriented. In order for individuals to lock their cars they need to press on the horn while pressing a button located discreetly on the muffler (no criminal would think of this) while their left foot touches the rear driver's side tire (*not* the passenger side) and their nose touches the rear view mirror with the air conditioner on. They need to stay in this position for only six minutes or until the car sounds an audible "lock-on" response. To turn off the alarm the driver simply has to do the same maneuver.

Convo-car—We don't know about you but we would think that most people like having others in their car. It's not that they don't like talking to themselves, but the answers they get back are sometimes, to put it nicely, expected. But Convo-car replaces the need for additional humans. Listen to this taped conversation:

Car:	Good morning.
Driver:	Good morning.
Car:	Please buckle your seat belt.
Driver:	Thank you. I will.
Car:	Wilma was right.
Driver:	What?
Car:	Last night's argument at 0:23:14:00 with the female human, Wilma.
Driver:	I don't want to talk about it.
Car:	You have no choice.
Driver:	Shut down.

Car:	If you weren't so cheap she wouldn't have ended up having to wash dishes with you at that restaurant.
Driver:	Cheap? I didn't want to pay because the-the, er, um…service was bad.
Car:	Take that!
Driver:	Oww! What was that?
Car:	Electro shock Lie detector.
Driver:	Abort! Abort! Shut down! Off! Off!
Car:	Tell the truth or I'm raising the volts.
Driver:	Okay, okay! I thought she was paying, okay?
Car:	Did she say so?
Driver:	No.
Car:	So why did you invite her out?
Driver:	I-I-
Car:	Take that!
Driver:	Owww! What was that for?
Car:	I detected a lie coming.
Driver:	Okay! Owww! I was hungry and broke alright?
Car:	Now you know why female Wilma is going to marry male human Jarred next year.
Driver:	Jarred? That guy with no neck?
Car:	Precisely. I hope you learned a lesson you petty human.
Driver:	Yeah. Stick with my bike. It doesn't talk back.

And thus a relationship is formed, a bond that will last for years to come (or until the driver goes crazy and flees the moving car…whichever comes first).

We've touched on a number of professional services but of course we couldn't touch on all of them. If you're in a position where you need to desperately fail write us a letter and we'll respond before 2005-why keep you waiting? But what is the goal that we seek in common? A return to the simpler things in life. A time when nobody knew you. A time when your burps weren't national news or a time when your running and tripping while going for a bus didn't turn into a national scandal and your ordering rose petal patties for dinner didn't cause the Dow to flip.

8

Success Stories

The AAMP (Association for Almost Made Profitters) is a 10 year old company set up for the sole purpose of helping companies out of the black and into the beige or red. Forrest Witochian who started this company was previously a temp in a larger firm, but through buyouts, resignations, downsizing and mutiny the company grew smaller but Forrest stayed on, becoming the president by default. So as the business diminished and dilapidated its direction changed and Forrest has brought it to the solid beige that it is.

This group has been set up for individuals who almost made a profit but were successfully saved from this monster. The names of the following individuals have been changed due to the potential embarrassment of said individuals.

TONY:

Tony ran a side shop deli, overpricing, understaffing and leaving the air conditioning on throughout the winter, his mind totally focused on mediocritous failure. But situations turned grim when he was reordering his Broccoli Cola supply. We'll let Tony tell us:

> "Yeah. I had just received my shipment of Broccoli Cola. The first batch was thrown away when the three year freshness time had expired. But on one particular day a customer walked in and ordered twenty. We had only twenty there, so in order to scare him

away, I boosted the normal price three fold to twelve dollars each. He was willing to give me fourteen dollars each! I fell into shock. The thought of making a profit scared me. Visions of me giving my employees raises, thus boosting them to minimum wage, danced menacingly in my head! Nightmares of putting something in the bank gave me a super migraine.

Fortunately I squeezed out the strength to call AAMP and they sent a representative over right away. He smoothly talked the customer into paying lower than the wholesale for the cans saving me from making a dreaded profit. I owe a lot to AAMP."

SYLVIA:

Sylvia's hair salon was a dismal success. This brought in celebrities, television series offers, book publishing offers and more. The stress from the glut of favorable press and movie offers sent Sylvia spiraling into stresstocrophy (very rare stress related illness-so rare, only Sylvia has it) One frantic call to AAMP was all that Sylvia needed. Sylvia tells us what happened next:

> "An AAMP representative came in almost minutes. He immediately changed my sign outside to read-"Only ugly need enter." He even made use of unused space and negotiated a morgue/hair salon concept which had an immediate effect. What added to its appeal is that even though there was a thick plastic partition that separated the two venues, it was clear enough to see all that was happening and add to the educational concept. He also brought video tapes of all the B movies the visiting celebrities starred in. And with a stroke of genius he put in "Scent de la Putrid" air fresheners around the office.
>
> In no time I was back in the beige (0 profit 0 loss) past the line of demarcation, back to the peace of mind I knew so well and the gradual relaxing move towards failure."

To date, in the ten years it has been set up, the AAMP has helped three people, two of them being mentioned in this chapter. This is one more than their goals indicated showing fine prospect potential to come.

9
Now What?

Now you're where you want to be. No striving for success, no pressures of staying ahead, no battling for recognition. But now you have a question. How do you provide for yourself and your family? There's a very simple answer: Find a job. We know you were trying to avoid the work-for-someone glut. But isn't that less stress than the life you've left behind? Of course! But now you're concerned with having to go on interviews and employment lines which are in themselves a full time job. Don't worry. This book is here to help you. Wouldn't it be nice to focus on something else other than that large man sitting next to you snoring mercilessly on your train ride to the city, or remain undistracted while that lady in front of you on the unemployment line scratches away at invisible flying irritants? To help you handle this task we have put together some mindioptics for you.

What are mindioptics? Mindioptics are basically the stimulation of visual thoughts. The word itself may sound very proquatious, but in reality it is a word that describes actions we do every day. For example: When you're walking to your favorite deli to get your asparagus Java, didn't you notice that old man walking along the edge of the sidewalk muttering something about the New York Knicks and the MSG conspiracy? Weren't you still able to concentrate on walking and eventually ending up at your destination? Then you were mindiopticizing. Mindiopticizing is the ability of the brain to carry out regular brain schisms while at the same time take a mental reprieve through external stimulus. Now, if the slightest distraction sends your brain in a frenzy and you suddenly can't walk properly because of not remembering if its left right left or right left right, then you are in serious trouble and this book would be too dangerous for you. But the average person should be relatively safe.

But why are the publishers of this book adding mindioptics to this work? These mindioptics aren't your average mindioptics. These were chosen specifically by mindiopticizers (those that create segregated mindioptics) for the sole purpose of providing a mental reprieve on your travel to that interview or unemployment line. While reading these carefully chosen subjects it will relax you mentally to face the day's challenges. *Additionally, personal insights from the author have been added, since it's his book.* This chapter has also been timed by Wait-Timer so as to coincide with the average unemployment line wait and train to interview travel time:

Why is it that movie animals are given screen names different from their real names? Is this to protect their identity? Does this help them with their motivation? Is this so they don't become typecast as…animals?

Why is it that the banks hire short old men to guard your money? Could it be a reverse psychological ploy to confuse would be bank robbers?

To Hug or not to Hurg. Out of all the many quimigulous displays of human affection, the hug is one of the most confusing. Though it's a simple gesture, it's been the catalyst behind fights, injuries, broken marriages and even death. According to the Organization for Understanding Chronic Hugimentation (O.U.C.H) legislation needs to be implemented to help individuals protect themselves from the many lawsuits that are being filed nationwide. Lawsuits stemming from unplanned kiss-hugs to hurgs (bone-cracking, cheek sucking hugs from grandparents) are rampant.

Margaret Fitchew, O.U.C.H. North East Region Sales division, helps us to understand this even more:

"When a hug is about to be given there are no signs from the receiver and the giver as to what kind of hug is about to be bestowed. One may be thinking that the other wants a Hug A complex (hug with a kiss) while the receiver of the hug reeks at the thought and is ready to give a Hug A simplex (no kiss). But because of their being no sign as to the type, confusion abounds. What also adds to this confusion, is that the giver may be a right cheek kisser (Hug A complex-right mode) while the receiver is a left kiss avoider (Anti-Hug A complex-left dodger) and thus they collide in the middle causing numerous nose contusions and hurt feelings."

"Many don't see the need for signs. We have petitioned the government to okay the distribution to the world market our Hug Notes which provide signs that anyone could use to let the other person know what they intend to do and what they don't intend to get, hugaciously speaking."

Richard Perry from our staff tearfully agrees with Margaret's comments.

"I feel the same way. I've been in situations where I was forced into a hug situation, but didn't know what to do. So I just kept my arms straight down while I was mugged, I mean, hugged. It was very traumatic because I wasn't ready, wasn't dressed for the hugging and I didn't know if this was a kiss hug or a bear hug."

How Richard feels is the way many individuals feel but are afraid to admit it. Right now injury waver forms, hug damage insurance and pre-hugtuals (pre-hug rights and requirements forms) are now being printed up. But according to our sources the Hug Notes should be available early 2003. Look out for it, but in the meantime, be very, very careful.

Here are some of the nation's commonest hug-induced collisions:

Person A's		Person B's
• Right cheek	into	left eye
• Left eye	into	chin
• Left shoulder	into	two front teeth
• Lips	into	ears
• Nose	into	right eye
• Right shoulder	into	open mouth
• Nose	into	underarm
• Left cheek	into	knee

Shouldn't we change those "Stop" signs to "Stop only for a while to see if the coast is clear and then go" signs. I was behind one driver who stopped, and stayed stopped for ten minutes (probably waiting for the sign to turn green which probably wouldn't have happened due to oxidation if he waited any longer).

Why are people so impatient? There was this one time when I had stopped at a red light. But as the light was turning (it was at the reddish-greenish phase) the guy behind me blew his horn. If it wasn't for the fact that my door was stuck and I would've had to wind down the passenger window to unlock the passenger side door to go around to open up my door...I would've given him a piece of my mind.

Do you have a problem with women? I do...why is it spelled "w-o-m-e-n" when it should be spelled "w-h-i-m-m-i-n" like it sounds? I know it may be too late now, but if I get a suitable answer I may reverse my lawsuit against my first grade teacher who organized that dreaded spelling bee.

How do some cars stay on the road? One car that was in front of me just screamed "get out the way, I'm gonna blow!" This car was shaking so much I could picture the driver dreading another reason to slow down ("oh, no…another stop sign" or "can't they move that wheel-chair any faster?"). He finally did stop in front of an immaculate house, which probably brought the real estate value down a couple of ten thousands. Before he got out he turned the car off (I know, I heard it click), but it took another ten minutes for the car to stop shaking. He had three bald tires and a training wheel which was kind of impressive. He didn't need a Club to protect the car because it would probably get stolen (the Club, that is). And it was the first one-door car I had ever seen. The passenger side door was not a door anymore, but it was now one big aluminum shield with a one foot diameter hole for air or roosting depending on the season.

After he climbed out his window he went to his trunk which in itself was a technological marvel; no keys necessary, no hinge necessary, just grunt and lift. Interesting. And the way the rust was designed (well, it seemed custom made) his fingers perfectly fit into its holes to help in the trunk removal/opening. He removed a bouquet of flowers, which were surprisingly clean, and brought it to the house.

After getting back into the car and starting it up…I just saw smoke and more smoke. I believe that that vehicle was probably the only human driven object that could be seen from the moon. The smoke was so bad that it created TAI (temporary artificial intelligence) in my car causing it to cough, spit and verbally threaten me for the first time. But after the smoke cleared his contraption was gone. I would of thought something mystical had happened to it if it wasn't for the small explosion that I heard a couple of blocks away that dictated otherwise.

Why is there such a thing as a disgruntled employee and not a gruntled one?

Built into every airplane is an aluminum housed, high temperature insulated, stainless-steel shelled, titanium armored, waterproofed, indestructible "black box" that can survive violent crashes and tons of pressure. Why don't they make the plane out of the same material?

How long before we throw away our favorite clothes? This has been an issue, especially for those that have a favorite pair of slacks.

One friend of mine loved his favorite slacks a little *too much*. He would wear these blue polyester boot cut monstrosities to job interview after job interview. He called it his "money" slacks (more like Russian rubles). I remember when he first bought them. The fabric appealed to him (and so did the 4/$12.99 price). In fact he liked it so much that even though he was a size 31 waist, this pant's size 45 waist didn't phase him. He finally found a seamstress who would do the "take in" job (and keep a straight face). When they finished the job he loved it (even though the "taking in" eliminated one pocket and brought the remaining pocket to the center of his butt).

Another thing, they were so short! It was so short that the slightest breeze almost revealed his calf. So short that after he got up from sitting he had to constantly pull them down to cover the purple top fringes of his corduroy blue socks (favorites too). Even his socks didn't like them. One time I thought I saw his socks pushing his slacks away, but it could've been my imagination. And the cuffs! A half-inch cuff is good. A one-inch cuff is just right. But a three and a half inch cuff was too much. I think he still had rain water in them from two days previous. But since he liked them there was nothing I could do.

How do you tell a perfect stranger that he has bad breath? Someone has to do it. I would think that as soon as they talk they would smell the raw emanation, embarrassingly excuse themselves and fix the problem. Only on Fantasy Island. After much research, I found out why it doesn't work that way.

First of all, once the stagnant breath is released it implants itself on an object, like your face, and *stays there afraid to move.* If you saw how this works through the magnifying glass you would be surprised likewise. They do not want to go back in! Their release is really an escape to freshness to rid themselves of the disgusting film that covers them. So once these fume molecules find there way on an unwilling victim, they transform their scents so as to become *unrecognized* by their sender and so the sender doesn't realize that it was his. Of course the receiver will feel the brunt because it's all new to their nose.

But what can you do? One man that sat next to me on a train had the worst breath I had ever *seen*. So there and then, while fighting nausea, I pulled out my pen, which barely survived this ordeal, and devised some options we can all use to help them, and preserve the mucus membranes of those that will be crossing their path:

- A smack

- Grab their nose and throw some mints inside their mouth. The mints may flee the initial time, but force them back in.

- The lean. Every time they talk to you, lean back as far as you can. Hopefully they get the hint before your back goes out.

- Scream and flee

- A dirty sock. A dirty sock is a natural enemy to bad breath in that they neutralize at least 60% of the fumungus bacteria. But only good quality fibers will work.

- The mass exodus (for workmates)

- Neighborhood petition

- Deodorant. This a very temporary solution, but make sure to use the spray as opposed to the stick.

- Mayoral warning

- Dirigible warning

- DeScent Detector. This object looks like a piece of paper with a tennis racket-like frame, but once held up to individual and bad breath is found, it changes colors to suit; yellow (barely detected) to mud green (the worst). $23.99 (includes face protector).

• Crop duster

• Kidnapping/electroshock treatment.

Why can't parents properly control their kids? Children are modern miracles. If as a kid I could've gotten away with what children get away with today, it would be a miracle. Now don't get me wrong. I love kids. In fact, I know a person who knows an individual who's related to someone that has a kid. But their cuteness has a limit. It shouldn't be an excuse for spoilazation.

When babies are born they honestly don't look so appealing. One baby was so ugly the doctors threw his food to him. Another baby was so ugly, the only way the parents got the dogs to play with him was by tying a steak around his neck. When some new parents on my block brought their baby over, I just had to ask the mother if she was sure she was holding it right side up. I had to. But in time he got cute, but then lost it again. When the child is at that precocious age spoiling is essential. But there has to be a cut off point. Parents need to unspoil them before it is too late. My unspoiling came at three. I learned responsibilities at that tender age: how to cook, mow, vacuum and light engine repair. But that is not the case today. And that is not the only thing that has changed since then. Discipline has definitely changed.

In my day parents had perfected the starestill technique…one stare, the children stood still. This skill was done to such a perfection that children could feel the very presence of their parent's peering eyes at up to 400 yards. But what has this been replaced with? "If you don't stop, you're not staying outside past 3 a.m.," or "If you don't behave, I'm limiting your allowance to $500 a week," or "If you don't clean your room you can only invite 120 to your rave party," or "If you don't eat all your beans I'm going to limit your visit to your online friend Floatingflesh to only a weekend" or the devastating, "You better behave or

I'm going to hide the remote under the red throw pillow so you have to walk all the way to the television to change channels!" Wow! Such threats! (faux horror). Parents should learn how to control their kids!

I was on the train one day when this family came on board led by a five year old. This five year old was definitely the man of the house. He decided where to sit and who sat where and whatever he chose all eight family members followed. In fact, an elderly woman was sitting in the seat this tyke wanted so he kicked and chased her to the other side of the train! His mother was so furious at what happened she kicked the elderly lady some more! I couldn't believe my eyes. Two against one! And the elderly lady wasn't even ready. This battle went on for about twenty minutes, but what was the horror of horrors was what happened next.

This young demon wanted to hold on to the straphanger loops. He stretched and stretched, but his stretching efforts didn't produce the accelerated tissue and skeletal generation that he desired (obviously not a bright five year old). So he grabbed a passenger by the ears and made him go on his hands and knees as this pint sized terror stood on his back and enthusiastically grabbed on to the loops. Afterward he sat on the passenger's back and pretended to be riding a bronco, kicking and pulling at their hair. I couldn't believe my eyes. I had just about enough of this brutality. I had to do something. I pushed the kid off my back and stood in front of his mother boldly and gave her a tongue lashing she would never forget not even minding the horrified looks of the other relatives around me.

But in hindsight, as I left the hospital later that evening, I kicked myself for even opening up my mouth, which wasn't a smart move after three hours of knee surgery. They don't make kids like they used to. Ouch.

Friends. *Who needs them?* We all do. But isn't it sad that the friends that we do find have a little too much cobwebs in the attic? That their elevator doesn't go all the way to the top? That their car's timing is a little off? That their thermometer is a tinge off normal? That their burger is a couple of degrees off well done? I guess you get the point (unless your elevator…forget about it). Why do I say this? Well, think of the last time your "friend" helped you out? Think back to that time at the basketball game. Here are you and your friend rooting for the Knicks along with a handful of the Garden crowd. In your zeal you spill your drink on the big, burly Knick fan next to you. He abruptly stops his cheering and gives you a look. But not just any look. His nose vibrates, smoke comes out his ears and you can count the red highways in his eyes as he stares you down like a hawk. You look at the spill which left a reddish dye on his corduroy capris and sneaks and you hurriedly try to sop it up with your tie. What does your friend do?

"What are you doing?" your friend whispers.

But of course your friend flunked Whisper 101.

"Don't let that galoot get his way."

Now you are in a bind. Your life or your friend. Which do you choose? You ease up on the cleaning which prompts Mr. Burly Fan to clear his throat so loud that it causes Shaquille O'Neal to miss a three-pointer. So you continue wiping off the fan's wet canvas high tops. But here goes your friend again:

"Don't be a wimp. Let him do it himself."

Mr. Burly Fan detects the whisper is about him and speaks up.

"What are you whispering about?"

Your "friend" says,

"My friend here is not taking any stuff from you. So you better clean yourself up!"

Looking at you, Mr. Burly shouts,

"Oh Yeah!"

And with a mighty hoist he lifts you up above the seats and shakes you menacingly. You reach for your friends shoulder or hand or *throat*, but he's gone. You somehow from the corner of your eye detect him across the stadium cheering on the Knicks. But before Mr. Burly could throw you courtside, an attractive voice coming from an attractive, short female distracts him.

"Hey, Leekman?"

Leekman drops you and runs to his pint sized cutie. They both leave arm in arm to your relief. So, once again your "friend" shows his true colors. But guess what? You'll be hanging out again, and laughing again and watching games again together. Maybe you need the help. And this isn't just for the males.

You females know exactly what I mean. What about the time you and your friend, Minerva went shopping together. She tries on a dress that is just too short. You mention it to her and after a couple of excuses she grudgingly acknowledges it. But the dress you try on is "perfect" to her.

"Honestly?" you ask.

"Yeah, honestly."

"Do you really mean it?"

"Out of all the dresses I have seen worn on any non-mannequin, this dress fits you like it was created just for you. It gives you exquisiteness that only a princess should have."

After your friend's gushing, you can't help but buy this dress. After-all, from your friend's response this dress would be the dress to elevate you to a status that has not been met by any living non-mannequin.

You can barely sleep as you think of the next day at work. When the day comes you jump out of bed and run straight to the closet. The doors practically open up themselves as you look for the dress. You take it out and do a little dance as you put it on the bed. Just the touch of the fabric gives you goosebumps. You prime yourself and practice your new dress inspired walk. As you put it on you instantly feel different. You feel like royalty. You feel like a countess getting ready to count her baubles in front of her trembling staff.

As you finish putting on the final touches you grab your briefcase (which coincidentally matches your shoes) and leave the house. Every eye is on you. You feel it. Traffic seems to slow down to view you in your exquisiteness and elegance. Homeless people throw money at you. Every green light turns red instantly along your path to the bus stop. As you get to the bus stop the bus which was screeching off is stopped at a red light. As you walk into the crowded bus, seats instantly appear free for you to sit down with an additional seat for your briefcase. When you get off at your stop the doors to your building automatically open (which you don't recall ever happening before). You gracefully walk to the elevator as individuals in the elevators clear it for you. The dress was working. The dress was working. You almost hear music coming from the skies just like in the movies.

When you get to your floor, you tickle yourself with the thought of the boss offering you a vice president position. As you walk in, all eyes look and stare. You try to feel humble, but humility was just going to have to take a back seat today. As you sit down at your cubicle you await the tons of phone calls coming in from staff and admirers wanting to find out about the new you. Before the phone could ring, though, you want to just give your splendid self another look. You run into the bathroom and primp and pose for forty-five minutes before gliding back to your station.

The red light on your phone shows that some voice mail was waiting for you:

"That is the ugliest garb I have ever seen in my whole life."
"Are you planning your funeral wear?"
"What animal is that? Platypus? Brontosaurus?"
"Wanted, escaped clown!"
"Sharon? Was that you on America's Most Wanted?"
"Women without taste...on the next Oprah."
"Are those hippo feathers around your neck?"
"Starvation Army had a sale?"
"I think you found the remedy for blindness."
"That dress would look good...under a canvas bag."
"I know a good doctor..."
"I got a couple of bucks..."

"Is that Extinct Wear?"
"Is this Derelict Week?"
"Hello? Sybil?"
"What are you protesting? Good taste."
"AAAAAAUUUGGGGGHHHH!!!!"
"Don't move-the ASPCA is coming now to remove that beast from your shoulder!"
"You're fired!"

After the last message you let out a blood-curdling scream that stills the mumblings of the office. You maniacally pick up the phone and punch your friend's number.

"Hello, Minerva?"
"Oh, hi. How are you?"
"Don't 'Hi Sharon' me! You told me that my dress was exquisite, that it fit me like it was made for me. You said it was the best you've ever seen on a non-mannequin. But ever since I got to work I've heard nothing but insults, raving mad insults. How could you do that to me? How? I trusted to you. I believed in you."
"I am not at my station right now. Please leave a message at the sound of the beep tone and I will return your call as soon as possible. [Beep]"
"AAAUUUGGGHHH!"

You somehow find a way to remain discreet throughout the day. Your staff mates considerately throw pizza over the cubicle walls for you at lunch time. But guess what? You will once again go shopping with your friend. You will once again hang out with her. This embarrassing debacle will become a distant memory. Why? We all need friends…and we all need help.

What is the one greatest enigma to face mankind? What is one topic that most people would love an answer for to have closure within themselves but have not yet found it? A survey of 270 homo sapiens gives us the answer:

10. Who's buried in Elvis' tomb?

9. What exactly happens when you sneeze with your eyes open?

8. Why do rats get such a bad rap and gerbils the good press?

7. If tomato seeds reap tomatoes and flower seeds reap flowers, what do birdseed reap?

6. Why is the pencil eraser located on the back of the pencil?

5. Why do smitten (love) and smite (death) sound like they have the same root word?

4. If a tree falls in a forest and no one is around, who has to wash the dishes?

3. What is Popeye *really* muttering to himself?

2. Why are there designs on the bottom of sneakers?

1. Who are "they"?

Yes. Who are "they"? Most of our lives have been dictated by the "they." For example: "You know what 'they' say, if you can't beat them, join 'em," or, "You know what 'they' say, the early bird catches the worm." Who are "they" and where did "they" come from? The answer is as scary as "they's" worldwide goal. So how did we get the inside scoop to this perplexing enigma? Journalist Micahel Tomatose has been covering stories like these for years. He was an assistant photojournalist on the famous Sock Theft mystery of 1973 and took the award winning pictures of Joseph "Sock Pilferer" Gunther with a purloined cotton knee-hi thus vindicating the washing machines in the North East Region. He was also present when the earliest known onion ring was unearthed in Medo Persia in 1988 *and* its theft by kamikaze chefs in 1989. But research on the "they" has been his most challenging and dangerous assignment. And as you will see, the very life of mankind is threatened.

Where to start? To print "they's" name properly we must print it T.H.E.Y. Yes, "they" is really an abbreviation for an underground group so sinister they make the Joker look like Alex Trebeck. These foreboding initials stand for Traveling Hindrance Environmental Yeomen. What is this sinister group up to? The answer will surprise you like it surprised us…kumquats. Yes, kumquats. But what does T.H.E.Y do that has anything to do with kumquats? Pay attention and learn about this sinister plot and what we need to do to stop them.

What T.H.E.Y researched about thirty years ago is how the human breath and elements surrounding it (e.g. speaking, and talking) has an affect on plant life. They found out in 1987 through ground-breaking experiments that man gives off carbon-dioxide while plants reciprocated with oxygen. But at the same time, research, initially distinct from their carbon-dioxide experiments, showed that kumquats are vegetables that hold a unique secret. They produce Tixotic Gas. Tixotic Gas is related to the gas cars need to run, but is even more potent. It was no surprise that they saw the huge monetary benefits of owning that technology. But to do it, they knew they had to corner the kumquat market. How? The answer came as the continued their experiments on oral gaseous secretions.

It was noted that certain words caused CO_2 to spring out at greater or lesser measures. But it was also noted that certain words produced CO_3, enough to slow the growth of the average plant *while at the same time causing the kumquat to thrive.* These levels of CO_3 releases are measured in quatoms. It was found that the more that people produced high levels of quatoms the greater the chance of floral stunting and kumquat growth.

Now, this is where it gets scarier (in a horticultural sense). In order for them to produce these at an exorbitant rate "they" had to devise words and phrases that increased the quatom rate. So from their research they saw that certain words produced more CO_3 than others. So they took these words, made phrases out of them and single-handedly spread them to as much people as they can, slowly choking the plant world while causing kumquats to grow in large numbers. But since no one took any notice of the larger than normal kumquat growth, the T.H.E.Y.s pillaged farms and stole kumquats to store so that they can sell them at exorbitant prices (which explains the rash of kumquat thefts going on worldwide)! In time, T.H.E.Y. would be the chief producer of kumquats and totally rule the fuel energy market. Such deviousness.

We will now see which phrases are doing the most damage to our planet while at the same time is helping the T.H.E.Y.s toward their ominous goals (these phrases far exceed the safe zone of 15—30 quatom level and should be avoided at any cost).

"You know what T.H.E.Y say..."

	Quatom Count
"...Look before you leap"	34
"...Don't count your chickens before they hatch."	50
"...Kuum sal esquibo phwen iggi mo ben, twentil cor" (...because a camel has a hump it doesn't mean it can't still use a good manicure)	72
"...Behind every woman is a good man."	75

And we can go on. We need to stay away from these crop destructing phrases if we know what is good for us and the well being of mankind.

Since press releases went out promoting the printing of his finding in this publication, Micahel has been missing. There are serious concerns that he may've been kidnapped and...kumquatted.

Who will you be glibulating over in the years to come? Glibulating? You're probably thinking, "Why would the publishers of this book, who through their excellent word usage, and diction, a credit to the English language, create such a fantastic word and mar the fine, upstanding example they have set to the publishing establishment?" Well, thank you for the compliment. But before you know it we just may be using that word in our daily language. In fact there just may be a lot of new gizmos added to our lives in the next coming years. We talked to several on our technological staff and got from them what they heard will be different in the years to come due to an onslaught of corporate mergers and takeovers:

• HiPfax
Hewlard Packard and a popular health provider will merge to manufacture portable fax machines which will soon be found on the person of the average business man and woman. But what makes theses unique is that the energy source will be located on a *internal* generator that is surgically built into the hip so while walking or fidgeting in REM sleep, you're generating power. Located right next to the cellular phone on the belt, it makes a nice, though heavy (19.5 lbs) portable office addition. A nose scanner is in the works.

• Lo-Jack Daniels
The maker of Lo-Jack and maker of the popular beverage will come together to protect beverage theft around the world. This technology is now being used in **Russia** and to date 4,567 pilfered wines have been returned. A U.S. release is now in the works.

• McViper
The popular burger chain will merge with the popular car protection product to protect burgers from fast food pilfers. This technology will

also be licensed out to competing chains. The need for this **protection** is seen especially on the job location where burgers are the most stolen lunch for the past 8 years. Example of audible warning:

"Get away from this bag. You are not the owner. I have a loaded packet of mayonnaise. Please stand back."

• Radio Steak
Radio Shack and a popular restaurant will team up to promote the first remote controlled steak. Just place your steak on a table (cleaned first) and at your control it will slink to you for an interesting and delicious meal. A hit at vegetarian gatherings.

• Burger Ting
When there's a good product there are always imitators. Due to the hit status of Radio Steak (above) Burger King's Burger Ting does the same thing. But while it also causes the meat to "walk," it has an additional feature. Through a chemical reaction of hollandaise sauce, Tabasco sauce and baking powder it lets off a "grrrr" sound that will definitely add spice to any table (while also creating a mass conversion to vegetarianism). Depending on the amount of baking soda added it could even produce a light foaming while in bun.

• Koduck
Kodak and the National Fowl Registry (NFA) will unite to produce the first down camera. Later models will have less feather displacement and an option that turns off the audible "quack" when pictures are out of focus.

• Home Despot
Home Depot and the Immigration Department will unite to provide a haven for overthrown monarchs and dictators where they will learn the fine art of cabinet making and wood framing. While a sanctuary away from their oppressed people, email access is still available.

• **New York Peppermint Pattie**

The popular mint company and the City of New York will combine to create the official New York mint. This mint will give biters the sensation of being stuck on an E train between stations during rush hour without air conditioning in the month of July standing next to a deodorant and mouthwash challenged street singer who does an on target imitation of Gilbert Godfreid singing Celine Deion.

• **Compaqt**

The world leader in computer sales will merge with Revlon and produce a compact for women that also allows them to read email while checking their face. Does not work in moving cars.

• **Dill**

The leader in Computer sales will merge with The Vlasic Pickle company and produce the first pickle powered computer. This will prove most necessary in countries where the use of traditional power (AC/ DC, generators, batteries, etc.) and meat power (bull, sheep, horse, etc.) is illegal.

• **Nikea**

The popular sneaker manufacturing company and the well known home interior establishment will collaborate to build homes that look like sneakers and inspired by famous NBA basketball players. Entrance into these phenoms can only be accomplished by shimmying up the shoelaces. Robbery is practically nill when the optional pump action sole protection devise is in place. The houses will range from the $10,000 Chris Dudley model to upwards of $900,000 for the Moses Malone model (which doesn't come with a ring).

• **Models**

In an effort to help all "over the hill" models, Models (formerly Modells, the leader in sports wear retail) will become the world leader of recycled models. These models, most in their early twenties will have their showcasing skills utilized once again through group door to door sneaker sales. Gate opening training, lighted walkway training and dog persuasion will be part of their academic initiatives. This opportunity, unlike the modeling they did previously, allows them to work up to 75 years of age with full benefits after retirement.

• Coalgate

It's been found that coal has decay-fighting properties and is added to the toothpaste market. An additional toothpaste will be developed to remove the oil and black deposits.

• ICan-on

The popular camera company and a successful motivational company will merge to produce traveling seminars that target the ever growing number of people who have a morbid fear of 50mm lenses.

• Rebook

Because of the steady increase of young people refusing to take off their sneakers (baths, bed, swimming, etc.) the popular sneaker manufac-turer will digitally imprint required reading into their sneakers. So instead of seeing red lights, each step will orate the works of Shakes-peare, Hamlet and MCHammer.

• Nintendons

Nintendo will team up with a board of physicians and make the hard-est, most vicious video game ever. So action packed that it comes with a free wrist surgery voucher from a local health care provider.

• Lelvis

The popular jeans company will merge with the Elvis House (home for depressed Elvis impersonators) and produce Lelvis Jeans. These jeans will look like Elvis' famous white, flared pants with all sales benefiting Elvis House.

• Gapp

The popular clothes manufacturer will preview their newest material, crabapple. Crabapple when seasoned and dried has been found to make a very durable cloth that stays strong from winter to spring, but tends to sprout, turn green and moldy and reek of a larvae luring smell before it falls apart in autumn.

• Pepsee
The soft drink champion and a popular eye care facility will bond together to promote their newest glasses. The traditional hour glass Pepsi bottles will come with removable bottoms which when added to the wire frames (located under cap) make a working, though slightly thick, pair of glasses. This newly formed company is currently squashing rumors that their proposed new glasses will cause burping of the eyes.

WORDS ARE A CHANGIN'

To think, some few years ago the term "computer virus" or "web surfer" didn't exist. Language, as is the norm, has been changing, but never at such a fevered pitch. This acceleration in articulation and the spittle discharge that ensues is mostly credited to the boon of technology. Our experts in entomological screenings have forecasted the next words on our plate:

tick	The person who always finishes your sentence for you.
glibulate	The way a person acts when they see formerly popular celebrities.
putrid slob	Neat and clean.
Wally	A person whose suits always find a way of exactly matching the office wallpaper.
squasm	A fake smile or grin.

...IT'S ABOUT THAT TIME

According to our WaitTimer meter you should be at the front of the line by now or walking into your potential employer's office for your first interview. If, though, you found yourself crumpled on the ground or laying on a passenger's lap in a fetal position or in a hospital room, *put this book down now!* You probably don't have the eugliotocticity to read and think at the same time. Don't worry, though we have other versions coming out for your convenience:

- Our simplified, illustrated version (6 pages)

- Our ReadNOW® service—For a small fee we'll read this book to you over the phone (for an additional fee you can have the Read-NOWexpress®service where we read this book *fast*).

- The "How To Fail" audiobook (seriously!)

10

Bonus Section!
Fail from the Start!

The resume. What if you get to the office for the interview and the stench of refried coffee hurts your senses? What if you find out upon entering the building that your junior high school basketball teammate who's still mad at you for missing the winning shot is the Vice President? Or, you walk into the office and there are others there who look like they *really* need the position you're applying for (e.g. begging, clinging to secretary, arm loads of apples, firstborn, etc.)? If you decide then and there that you're going to find another job elsewhere, should you run out screaming? No. The key? Having a secondary, or escape-resume.

The resume, as you know, has a number of portions. You have ten seconds for your resume to be scanned and either accepted or rejected. So which area gets the first three seconds? Your Objective. Your Objective, which appears at the top of each resume, allows the peruser to "see" you without actually seeing you. What can you put as your escape-resume's Objective that will not only trigger an involuntary gastroesophageal reflux but will also quickly dismiss any thoughts of your ever being contacted?

> Objective: Seeking employment where I can steal pencils, papers and any unanchored office utensils.

Objective: Seeking employment where I can use their office equipment to work on the great American novel.

Objective: Seeking employment where I can use their computer to play the latest video games while under the guise of work.

Objective: Seeking employment where I can work for a time, raid the boss' desk, get myself fired and apply for unemployment.

Objective: Seeking work where I can enhance my skills while at the same time sneak into payroll and make some "adjustments."

Objective: Seeking a firm that doesn't protect their employees' lunch.

Objective: Seeking a company where I can make all the long distance calls I want to Bulgaria.

But let's say that you didn't bring your escape-resume. The interview is the next step. How can you fail the interview to the point of having your resume entered into the circular file of infamy? We have a number of graduates from our online courses below. Look carefully at their style and learn. If done properly you will make the interviewer's day as he triumphantly dismisses you, slams the door and dumps your resume. He would be happy that he protected the office from such an un-corporate stench (and also have bragging rights to that feat). Let's look at Ed in action.

Interviewer: Mr. Ed Watchinsky, nice to meet you.

(Shaking hands)

Ed: It's my pleasure. No one has told me before in my whole life that it's nice to meet me. In fact one day in kindergarten this one girl was so nice. Her name was Elizabeth. But I think she was after my lunch box. I had the best lunch box in the whole school. She would take out my lunch, throw it on the ground and put hers in it and give me a little kiss on the cheek. It took me years to realize that it wasn't me but my box she was after. But I learned my lesson. I don't lend my lunch box out. In fact I have it here with me...

Interviewer: Er, um...Mr. Watchinsky, can you let go of my hand?

Ed: Oh, sorry. That's a nice tie. Thirty years ago I had a tie like that, but it was fluorescent and...

What about **Minerva**?

Interviewer: Ms. Minerva Washington? Nice to meet you.

(Shaking hands)

Minerva: Why are you shaking my hands like that?

Interviewer: Sorry. I'm just being friendly. Just a simple handshake.

Minerva: Oh. You think I can be swayed by your fine double breasted suit and your alligator shoes? What kind of woman do you think I am?

Interviewer: Oh...sorry. If you can please have a seat.

Minerva: A leg man, eh? No way you seeing my knees! I'm not the corporate cutie you're looking for. If you want to see knees, Mr. Moneybags, go to the zoo!

Let's see how Bartholomew impresses...

Interviewer: Mr. Bartholomew Rivers?

(Shaking hands)

Bartholomew: W-who wants to know?

Interviewer:	No. Just repeating your name.
Bartholomew:	Oh.
Interviewer:	I see you have an interesting resume.
Bartholomew:	It's all true I tell ya. It's all true.
Interviewer:	Oh. I'm not questioning the veracity of this information—
Bartholomew:	So what are you questioning? It wasn't me I tell ya! It wasn't me!

Let's listen in on Rafael as he talks to this female interviewer…

Interviewer:	Mr. Rafael DuSuave? Nice to meet you.
Rafael:	I know. The pleasure is all yours.

(Shakes interviewer's hands while also massaging her elbow)

Interviewer:	Er, um…So Mr. Rafael, what made you decide to look into our firm?
Rafael:	I was looking for a company that has women as beautiful as yourself to cater to me.
Interviewer:	Excuse me. I didn't need that whispered in my ear.
Rafael:	Sorry. Just showing you my interpersonal skills.
Interviewer:	Mr. Rafael, I think this interview is over.
Rafael:	Yes, I know. I knew that all this resume talk would pale eventually. We both know that you want to go someplace quiet with me so you can tell me how exquisite a find I am.
Interviewer:	Out! And take your silk resume with you!

Jermaine: Art at work.

Interviewer:	Mr. Jermaine Richardson? Nice to meet you.
(Shakes hand with tissue)	
Jermaine:	T-Thank you.
Interviewer:	Your resume is very impressive. Any questions before we continue?
Jermaine:	Yes. Did you wash your hands?
Interviewer:	Excuse me?
Jermaine:	You handle a lot of resumes don't you?
Interviewer:	Yes, that is one of my assignments.
Jermaine:	Did you know resume-borne diseases are the primary cause of immature death among interviewers ages 24–49?
Interviewer:	Er, um, no.
Jermaine:	That clip on tie you have there is made of polyester fibers, right?
Interviewer:	Er, um, yes, I think.
Jermaine:	It is. In fact I smell a combination of polyester and rayon. Those are natural enemies. The inherent fiber clash can release overbearing and sometimes life threatening scents.
Interviewer:	Well, thanks for the info. About this employment opportunity…
Jermaine:	That toupee isn't made out of natural hair.
Interviewer:	Why you—
Jermaine:	Natural hair is better and it releases a less smelly follicle discharge. It may also contribute to scalpatial banding.

Interviewer:	Next!

Owen, a walking masterpiece of creativity.

Interviewer:	Mr. Owen Tochins?
(Shakes hands)	
Owen:	Thank you.
Interviewer:	Your resume is very interesting, especially the part about your kindergarten accomplishments. But under employment history it doesn't say anything . Do you have what it takes to be a capable part of this firm?
Owen:	The years of work I have done in your company's field of expertise and the wisdom I have acquired over the years cannot be put into words. On my last nineteen jobs I excelled to degrees that brought nothing but awe and respect from my comrades. The expertise I have attained to will make me a perfect candidate for your establishment. After looking into your company's history I am confident that I can take your company from the dismal level that it is to a level you have only dreamed of due to my quest for excellence in the field and my desire to take what I know, add it to what you *wish* you knew and carry your establishment further.
Interviewer:	That's er, ah…interesting. Do you have any questions?
Owen:	Yes. What do you do here?
Interviewer:	Wow. Something you didn't know. Next!

Now, keep in mind. To be this good didn't come naturally. Owen, for example, didn't always have the expertise he has. He served a minor stint in jail for impersonating a fire hydrant, but has wonderfully bounced back. He is now working at a rubber bagel supply house in Washington. If he could be where he wants to be and be happy…you can too.

Onward to the Future

Now you've reached the end of this book (which should be obvious). In these few chapters we have seen what is needed to reach failure success while at the same time preparing you for your upcoming career in any job you see fit to add your skills to. But bear in mind, these points, though well researched may, even though it's rarely the case, bring you monetary success as opposed to the wished upon opposite. If success does abound, we apologize. Re-read the chapters again and try and try until you un-succeed. If you continue hitting success after success, you can email the publishers at troyangles@hotmail.com for further advice. Even though our advice is free, there is a fee for using one of our already limited supply of synapses to assist you in your request, but that can be discussed online.

What is our future? We will continue to bring you ground-breaking stories, riveting exposes and necessary insights. We will not pander to the baser instincts of the masses with subjects about health, family and science. Look for us as we prepare to *possibly start thinking* about our future publishing efforts, which may include some of the following:

Prunes: Your link to the future

The Corn Flakes Chronicles: Can't we get a full box?

Michael Jordan: "It was all camera tricks"

Elvis: "I'm Back"

The Memory: Remember More Through Exercise

Mars: The Acne On The Face-Ancient Condos?

The Thumb-Do we really need it?

The Memory: Remember More Through Exercise

So, until next time, take care and happy failing!

Central-One Publishing
troyangles@hotmail.com
(888) 343-676

Afterword

Dear Readers:

We will now take this opportunity to be serious, a feat that was successfully attempted fourteen years ago. Even though it was the roughest ten minutes of our lives we will attempt this again for the benefit of our new readers. Wish us well:

> The statements, quotes, surveys, names, technologies, stocks, information about famous people, and everything else in this book is entirely fictional. Where names are used, these names were selected randomly from the mind of the publishers and were not intended to represent anyone. Where celebrity names are used, these are said with no intent to harm or embarrass (they can, and have been doing that on their own without any help from us).

Conclusions

NO PENCILS WERE HARMED DURING THE
PUBLISHING OF THIS PUBLICATION

About the Author

There's really not much to be said about me. I'm an idea man. I like to think about new ways, new thoughts, new ideas and different way of seeing things. But what makes this thoughtification process even more enjoyable is when I can bring them to life. This book is an example.

I would like, though, to give special thanks to all that had a help in this publishing effort. If your name deserves to be here and is not, my humble apologies.

Corey Burkes
Fiona Rowe
Davida Williams
Annazette Norville
Elida Martes
Perline Stoddart
Ivor McGee
Syntychia Kendrick
Sharon Chambers
Dan Black
Andrea Love
iUniverse

Look out! There are more thoughts, ideas, and frivolous traquitations to come!

Troy Remington Dowden

0-595-25735-6

www.ingramcontent.com/pod-product-compliance
Lightning Source LLC
Chambersburg PA
CDIIW021543200526
45163CB00015B/1146